Does Your Church
Have a Prayer?

Does Your Church Have a Prayer?

In Mission toward the Promised Land

PARTICIPANT'S GUIDE

Marc D. Brown | Kathy Ashby Merry | John G. Briggs Jr.

DISCIPLESHIP RESOURCES

P.O. BOX 340003 • NASHVILLE, TN 37203-0003
www.discipleshipresources.org

Cover design by Christa Schoenbrodt
Interior design by PerfecType, Nashville, TN

ISBN 13: 978-0-88177-567-9

Library of Congress Control Number: 2009922557

Contents

Preface

Fellow disciples of the risen Christ,

You are about to embark on a six-week Bible study that will allow your voice to be heard. *Does Your Church Have a Prayer? In Mission toward the Promised Land* is an intentional process of spiritual engagement that your church is conducting to empower your community of Christian disciples to make decisions about your present and future ministries based on certain biblical principles. Through this study, you will:

- Learn about God's Promised Land for disciples of Jesus;
- Hear how the story of the twelve spies who presented a report about God's Promised Land to the congregation of Israel tells the story of today's church;
- Identify the giants that are dwelling in the Promised Land God envisions for your community of faith;
- Understand where to find true power and ask right questions about your congregation;
- Learn how the biblical principle of *Beyond and Within* can transform the identity of a congregation;
- Discover why it is essential for members of a congregation to have the mind of Christ among them if they wish to enter God's Promised Land for Jesus' disciples.

As you learn the biblical principles that are part of this study, you will be responding to questions that other members of your congregation will also be answering as they participate in this Bible study. The answers to these questions will formulate information that will allow members of your church to make intentional decisions about the nature and mission of your life together. At the conclusion of this Bible study, members of your church will hold a congregational meeting and present a report about the responses for reflection and feedback. In turn, members of your church will envision a congregational plan for mission and ministry based on the consensus of your community of Christian disciples.

The premise of this Bible study is that God calls every congregation to dwell in God's Promised Land for Jesus' disciples. If a congregation wishes to enter and live faithfully in God's Promised Land, however, its members must make choices that will affect their present and future lives.

Joshua 24 tells the story of the congregation of Israel making intentional choices about their present and future lives. Having entered God's Promised Land, their leader Joshua has assembled the twelve tribes of Israel at Shechem to present themselves to God. Verses 1-13 are a recounting of the stories of faith and of wandering that had formed them as they responded to God's vision of faith through Abraham. Beginning with verse 14, they are called to renew their covenant of faith as they live in God's Promised Land.

> Now fear the LORD and serve the Lord with all faithfulness. Throw away the gods your forefathers worshiped beyond the River and in Egypt, and serve the LORD. But if serving the LORD seems undesirable to you, then choose for yourselves this day whom you will serve, whether the gods your forefathers served beyond the River, or the gods of the Amorites, in whose land you are living. But as for me and my household, we will serve the LORD.

> Then the people answered, "Far be it from us to forsake the LORD to serve other gods! It was the LORD our God himself who brought us and our fathers up out of Egypt, from that land of slavery, and performed those great signs before our eyes. He protected us on our entire journey and among all the nations through which we traveled. And the LORD drove out before us all the nations, including the Amorites, who lived in the land. We too will serve the LORD, because he is our God."

> Joshua said to the people, "You are not able to serve the LORD. He is a holy God; he is a jealous God. He will not forgive your rebellion and your sins. If you forsake the LORD and serve foreign gods, he will turn and bring disaster on you and make an end of you, after he has been good to you."

> But the people said to Joshua, "No! We will serve the LORD."

> Then Joshua said, "You are witnesses against yourselves that you have chosen to serve the LORD."

> "Yes, we are witnesses," they replied.

> "Now then," said Joshua, "throw away the foreign gods that are among you and yield your hearts to the Lord, the God of Israel."

And the people said to Joshua, "We will serve the LORD our God and obey him" (Joshua 24:14-24, *NIV*).

The time has come for your congregation to gather at Shechem as you make intentional choices about your present and your future. As you prepare to answer the call of God's Promised Land for your church, what choices shall you make? To whom will you yield your hearts?

Bible Study Leader Instructions

Thank you for agreeing to be a six-week Bible study leader for *Does Your Church Have a Prayer? In Mission toward the Promised Land*. As a Bible-study leader, you will help the voice of the people in your community of faith to be heard as your church develops a strategic ministry plan. You will also help people in your church to know each other better through a small-group setting designed to help them grow in their faith.

As a Bible-study leader, you have the following responsibilities:

- be supportive of the visioning process that your church's governing body has approved.
- Instruct the participants to bring their Bibles to each study session as scriptures will be read each week.
- Begin each study session with the following covenant prayer:

Holy God, you created us out of your love for humankind. It is out of your love for us that we have accepted your grace and chosen to follow Jesus, proclaiming the risen Christ. As Jesus' disciples, we know it is your desire for all the people of the world to be reconciled to you and one another for the redemption of all creation.

We gather as your people now and give you thanks and praise for your presence in our lives. We give thanks for the ways in which you have guided and blessed this congregation. We seek your will and guidance. Holy God, we gather to listen and discern together as we covenant to follow Jesus for your glory. Amen.

- Be a neutral facilitator of discussion based on weekly Bible-study material through group participation and responses to questions. (Participants should read Bible studies before the actual time of gathering.) There are three areas of responses:

1. Group reflection on the scripture passages for each study: Questions for Scriptural Reflection;

2. Recording responses of participants that will provide assessment information regarding the current reality of your church: (Helping Your Voice To Be Heard). You will submit these responses to Small-Group Bible Study Coordinator;

3. Thought and conversation within the study group: Questions for Reflection and Discussion. As a facilitator, your role is to encourage responses without dominating or unduly influencing group discussion. Depending upon the number of people in your study group, you may wish to invite people to speak in pairs as they respond to questions.

Begin and end the study session on time. Each Bible study should last for a maximum of ninety minutes. If you have specific questions regarding your responsibility as a Bible-study leader, you should contact your Small-Group Bible-Study Coordinator. May God's blessings be with you in this important ministry of spiritual engagement for your church.

Does Your Church Have a Prayer?

Does your church have a prayer? The seventeenth chapter of John records Jesus' prayer for your church and for all communities of Jesus' disciples who stand on the edge of God's Promised Land.

God's Promised Land for Jesus' Disciples: John 17:1-26

Jesus prayed for your church! Jesus prayed for you!

Envisioning a reality where the truth of God's love would guide his disciples, Jesus prayed. Preparing for his crucifixion in a fallen creation and for his resurrection in the redemption of a new creation, Jesus prayed. Praying for his disciples who followed him in his earthly ministry and his disciples who would follow him in his resurrected ministry, Jesus looked over into God's Land for his disciples. In this Promised Land, Jesus' disciples have their lives shaped by the reality of their Savior's crucifixion and resurrection as they live in the dawning of a new day.

Looking over into God's Promised Land for his disciples, Jesus prayed was that the power of divine love that was sending him to Calvary would form his disciples. There is a biblical word for this forming power of God's love: sanctification. Sanctification speaks of the empowering presence of God that helps followers of Jesus to live in the vision of Jesus' prayer for them. Sanctification empowers Christians to live in the wholeness of God's vision for their lives as revealed through the truth of Jesus' life, death, and resurrection. It is this vision that empowers Christians to allow their lives to be shaped by the love that guided Jesus to the cross.

Sanctification is the vision of Jesus' prayer for his disciples in John 17:17-19 as he said, "Sanctify them in the truth; your word is truth. As you have sent me into the world, so I have sent them into the world. And for their sakes I sanctify myself so that they also may be sanctified in truth." An act of God's searching and sending grace, sanctification describes the nature of God's Promised Land for Jesus' disciples. In this Promised Land, Jesus' followers are empowered to look beyond themselves and live as people who are sent into the world through the power of God's love. It is through sanctification that followers of Jesus grow and mature in their faith as they are re-created in the image of Christ.

Remembering the truth of divine love that led Jesus to Calvary, Jesus' disciples are connected with the saving power of Jesus' crucifixion and resurrection. With their lives shaped by the truth of the cross, they remember who God is calling them to become as their lives are connected to the biblical story of faith. They understand that this story is about God, who will not turn away from the goodness of creation. Living in God's Promised Land for Jesus' disciples, their lives bear witness to the that the power of the God of creation is greater than the power of a fallen creation.

Joy and unity are the milk and honey of God's Promised Land. These are the qualities that define the nature of Jesus' disciples when they are created and formed in the image of Christ. Jesus prayed for joy for his disciples in 17:13: "But now I am coming to you, and I speak these things in the world so that they may have my joy made complete in themselves."

Joy is the second fruit of the Holy Spirit listed in Galatians 5:21. Joy gives evidence of the presence of the Holy Spirit in a Christian's life. As Jesus prepared himself for the agony of the cross, he prayed that his followers would be made complete in his joy. These two realities, crucifixion and joy, may seem like an odd pairing, but they are both fruits that are found in God's Promised Land.

Crucifixion is the reality of a biblical principle entitled *Beyond and Within*. More will be said about the reality of crucifixion and this biblical principle in the fifth chapter of this Bible study. In understanding Jesus' prayer for joy, however, it is important to note that Jesus' disciples find joy in the reality of Jesus' obedience to the cross. It is this divine obedience that allows Christians to understand that joy is the result of a life that witnesses beyond itself. One of the radical revelations of Jesus' prayer for joy is that evidence of the fruit of the Holy Spirit may be present even in situations that may not be defined as joyful.

For the Christian, joy is not found in personal acts of self-satisfaction but instead in the truth of God's redeeming act of a common salvation through Jesus Christ. One biblical witness to this act of common joy and salvation is found in Hebrews 12:1-2:

> Therefore, since we are surrounded by so great a cloud of witnesses, let us also lay
> aside every weight, and sin which clings so closely, and let us run with perseverance
> the race that is set before us, looking to Jesus the pioneer and perfecter of our faith,
> who for the joy that was set before him endured the cross, despising the shame, and
> is seated at the right hand of the throne of God.

The good news of redeeming faith is that Christians are able to participate joyfully in God's act of redemption through Jesus Christ. Our joy is not limited to the temporary. Connected to the faith that has been shared with us and the faith which we share, we are living witnesses as we join the cloud of witnesses for whom Jesus prayed in John 17:20: "I ask not only on behalf of these, but also on behalf of those who will believe in me through their word."

It is through a shared or communal joy in the redeeming faith of Jesus that Jesus' disciples may be united in the glorifying wholeness of God's vision for life. Jesus prayed that his disciples would be united in the glory that God had given him: the glory of living as a Savior who was sent to let the world know the God of love. Living as this Savior, Jesus, in turn, has given this same glory to his followers. It is this gift of glory that unites Jesus' disciples to live as people who are sent to let the world know that God's love is revealed in the life, death, and resurrection of Jesus.

Jesus prayed for unity for his disciples in John 17:22-23 as they lived the message of God's love he had been sent to share: "The glory that you have given me I have given them, so that they may be one, as we are one, I in them and you in me, that they may become completely one, so that the world may know that you have sent me and have loved them even as you have loved me."

Love in the Christian community is a calling beyond self-focus. The first fruit of the Holy Spirit in Galatians 5:22, love witnesses to the "sending" power of God through Jesus. As members of a churches live in the "sending" power of God's love, they are united through a divine vision of the cross that calls them to a communal life beyond the pettiness and grumblings that can sometimes dominate the culture of a congregation. This divine vision leads to intentional ministry where the spirit of the congregation is defined by a sense of mission and hope. The sad reality, however, is that some congregations, instead of being bound for God's Promised Land for disciples of Jesus Christ, choose to wander in the wilderness of life defined by the absence of joy, the presence of self-focus, and a lack of meaning. This is not the reality for which Jesus prayed as he prepared himself for the cross. The glad reality is that congregations can be bound for the Promised Land. Living in the reality Jesus envisioned, their members are able to live in the hopeful joy of a Promised Land where the stories of their lives are united in telling the truth of God's divine love revealed through Jesus Christ. The cross of Jesus Christ defines their life together.

Missional qualities define the communal lives of congregations that are bound for God's Promised Land as their members focus beyond themselves by:

- glorifying God through their faith in Jesus (verse 10);
- understanding their call as people who are being sent into the world (verse 18);
- making God's love known through Jesus (verse 26).

Jesus' life and ministry had one intention: to glorify God. It was this intention that guided Jesus' prayer that the Father would be honored through the Son and that the Son would be honored through the Father in the hour of his crucifixion. Praying as a Savior sent on a mission, Jesus focused beyond himself.

Followers of Jesus have one purpose for their lives and ministries: to glorify God. It is this purpose for which Jesus prayed as he focused beyond his own concerns to the concerns of his followers. Focusing beyond themselves, Christian disciples honor God as they understand their call as people who are being sent by Jesus into the world. This calling is manifested in acts of faith that witness to the power of God's love revealed through the cross of Jesus Christ. Through acts of faithfulness that point beyond their own concerns, congregations of disciples can become transforming symbols of God's presence to people who are searching for purpose in their lives.

From Jesus' prayer, we understand that the Promised Land of discipleship occurs as Jesus' followers live in the unity of community. In the New Testament, the word that describes the community of Jesus' disciples is *church*. Through the corporate life of the church, disciples of Jesus Christ live out the nature and mission of Jesus' visionary prayer.

Nurtured and equipped by the reality Jesus envisioned, effective ministry in the church is defined by how people align themselves to the nature and mission of Jesus' prayer. In the book *Grace Matters*, Chris Rice tells of his experiences with a church called Voice of Calvary in Jackson, Mississippi. Voice of Calvary is a church that sponsors ministries for college interns from around the country. Chris traveled from Vermont to Mississippi to be a three-month intern in 1981 and left in 1998. During that time he became a friend and yokefellow in ministry with Spencer Perkins. Spencer was the son of John Perkins, a civil-rights leader in Mississippi and the founding pastor of Voice of Calvary. Chris was Euro-American. Spencer was African-American. Together, they partnered in a ministry of friendship and reconciliation.

One day, Chris and Spencer spoke to a group of college interns who had traveled to Jackson, Mississippi, to share in the ministry of Voice of Calvary Church. Spencer had these words of advice to share about their faith in Jesus Christ: "Christianity ain't between you and God. It's about joinin' in God's agenda and becomin' part of a new people—a body that together witnesses God's truth to the world." [1]

As members seek to envision a future defined by God's agenda, they need to remember that they are connected to the story of God's love defined through Jesus. Guided by divine possibilities, a local church is called to remember the nature and mission of Jesus' prayer. If the nature of a church is sanctified by joy as it is united in the love of Jesus, it will enter God's Promised Land of discipleship. If the mission of a church glorifies God as its members are unified in living as people sent into the world to make God's love known, it will enter God's Promised Land of discipleship. Should a church forget the nature and mission of God's agenda, the result will be wandering in search of a reason for existence.

Believers in Jesus Christ are connected to a story of redeeming grace that is greater than the individual stories of their lives. Joining the stories of individual lives with the story of God's love in Jesus, the Church offers the possibility for transformation of life as disciples of Jesus join in God's agenda. Understanding that Jesus' call to discipleship is an invitation to join in God's story of salvation, disciples of Jesus answer their Savior's call upon their lives. They understand God's Promised Land of discipleship is possible only as they live as communities of faith in the vision of Jesus' prayer for them, "a body that together witnesses God's truth to the world." These are churches that align themselves to the envisioned reality of Jesus' prayer as they live in the vision of joy and unity in Jesus to the glory of God and the mission of being followers of Jesus sent into the world.

Does your church have a prayer? Jesus' prayer in John 17 has already answered that question. Will your church live in the reality of Jesus' prayer? This is a question that members of your community of faith will need to answer for themselves. God's Promised Land of discipleship awaits your response.

Praying Together

> God of all love and redeeming grace, we give you thanks for your call to be followers of Jesus in this age. We especially praise you for Jesus, who prayed for us, and who prays for us still. We ask that through these prayers of Jesus we will gain a heightened sense of your leading. Grant us obedient hearts that we might be your faithful disciples to the world. As we begin our journey to your Promised Land of discipleship, fill us with your renewing presence that we might find clarity and unity in your perfect purpose. In the name of Jesus, the Christ, we make this prayer. Amen.

Seeking God's Vision Together

The following questions provide an opportunity for personal and group reflection as your church seeks God's vision. The three types of questions will lead you to:

- *Reflect on the Scripture passages of the study (Questions for Scriptural Reflection);*
- *Express your opinion regarding the current reality of your church (Helping Your Voice To Be Heard);*
- *Participate in thought and conversation (Questions for Reflection and Discussion).*

Questions for Scriptural Reflection

From the scriptural texts in this chapter, reflect on the following questions and answers:

1. For whom did Jesus pray?

   Verse 20: For both the disciples who followed Jesus in Jesus' earthly ministry and for the disciples who will believe in Jesus through their word. This means Jesus prayed for you and your church.

2. What were the purposes of Jesus' prayer?

> *Verse 13: That the joy of Jesus may be made complete in Jesus' disciples.*
> *Verse 17: That Jesus' disciples may be sanctified in the truth of God.*
> *Verse 22: That Jesus' disciples may be one as Jesus and the "Heavenly Father" are one.*

3. What is the mission of Jesus' disciples?

> *Verse 10: To glorify God through Jesus.*
> *Verse 18: To be sent into the world.*
> *Verse 26: That the love of God made known in Jesus may be known in Jesus' disciples.*

4. What words in Jesus' prayer in John 17 indicate that Jesus actually prayed for YOU?

> *Verses 20-22: Jesus prayed for his disciples who would follow him in his resurrected ministry through the witness of the disciples who followed him in his earthly ministry.*

Helping Your Voice To Be Heard

Responses to these questions will formulate information that will lead your church to make intentional decisions about the mission and ministry of your life together. Please enter your responses in the corresponding section of the response sheet provided with this study book. Each answer should be your initial response.

1. Would you consider your church to be a praying church?

   a. Yes;

   b. No.

2. Is your church a joyful place?

   a. Yes;

   b. No.

3. Does a common vision that glorifies God unite your church?

   a. Yes;

   b. No.

4. Do people believe in Jesus because of your church?

   a. Yes;

   b. No.

5. Does your church make God's love known?

   a. Yes;

   b. No.

6. Does your church have a vision/mission statement?

   a. Yes;

   b. No.

7. If your church has a mission statement, do you think it reflects the mission of Jesus' prayer for his disciples as noted in question three of "Questions for Scriptural Reflection"?

   a. Yes;

   b. No.

8. Which question would generate the most discussion at your church?

   a. Who has the keys to which doors at your church?

   b. How can we open the doors of our church to our community?

Questions for Reflection and Discussion

The answers to the following questions provide an opportunity for personal and group reflection as your church seeks God's vision. These questions will help you to know more about your church and each other.

1. What difference does it make to know that Jesus prayed for you and your church?

2. What are the characteristics of a praying church?

3. Are the characteristics of a praying church evident in your faith community?

4. Describe a time you have felt especially joyful at church. What made that a joyful time for you?

End Notes

1. Chris P. Rice, *Grace Matters: A Memoir of Faith, Friendship, and Hope in the Heart of the South* (San Francisco: Jossey-Bass, 2002) 110.

What Reality Do You Choose?

What reality do you choose? The answer your church gives will either lead your congregation to God's Promised Land or to the wilderness. Numbers 13:1–14:9 is an analogy of today's church as we stand on the edge of the Promised Land Jesus envisioned in his prayer for his disciples in John 17.

Exploring the Promised Land: Numbers 13:1–14:9

God's Promised Land was ready. People whose only experience of reality had been slavery were waiting. Moses and Aaron were waiting. All that was required was a faithful report from the twelve spies appointed by Moses to go to the Promised Land and bring back a realistic and encouraging report of what lay ahead for the children of Israel. For forty days, this "Promised Land Task Force" inspected the land God had promised to Abraham in Genesis 12 and 17. For forty days, the people waited for a report on God's promise of a new day and a new home. Finally, the spies returned with their reports.

They were in consensus about the potential of the reality they saw: a land that was beyond anything they had ever imagined. To confirm their report, they brought back visible, tangible evidence of the possibilities that were ahead. From the Valley of Eshcol, they had cut down a branch with a single cluster of grapes, and they carried it on a pole between two of them. What they saw was so wonderful that they told Moses, Aaron, and the congregation that the Promised Land flowed with milk and honey. They were also in consensus about the challenge of the reality they saw: the people dwelling in the Promised Land were strong, lived in large fortified cities, and of great size.

The twelve spies agreed on the reality they had seen and they were consistent in their report of the possibilities and challenges of the Promised Land. It was here, however, that they gave two different interpretations of their reports. The interpretations differed because of how these appointed spies interpreted reality.

Reality is the present experience of life. Numbers 13:1–14:9 teaches that there are two ways we can interpret the present experience of life. One possible interpretation is *Perceived Reality*. This interpretation occurs when perceptions of past experiences and subsequent fears of the future control a person's response to the present. Another possible interpretation of the present experience of life is *Envisioned Reality*. This interpretation occurs when God's promised future controls a person's response to the present. Perceived Reality leads you on a journey to the wilderness. Envisioned Reality leads you on a journey to the Promised Land. The response of the ten spies and of the congregation of Israel to the reality of the giants in the Promised Land is an example of Perceived Reality. The response of Joshua and Caleb is an example of Envisioned Reality.

Perceived Reality

The perceived reality that controlled the response of the ten spies and the of congregation of Israel is found in Numbers 13:33. Reporting on the reality of giants in the Promised Land, the ten spies told the congregation, "to ourselves we seemed like grasshoppers, and so we seemed to them." These are significant words. They reflect how the spies perceived themselves as they faced the challenge of the giants who dwelled in the Promised Land. Feeling inadequate to meet the challenge before them, they began to focus on the inadequacy of their own self-perceptions rather than on the promised future that God had given to Abraham. These spies' vision of the future could not see beyond the present reality of the giants who dwelled in the Promised Land nor could their vision see beyond themselves. As a result, the spies' present perception of seeming like grasshoppers to the giants and to themselves controlled their response to the future that God had promised.

The congregation of Israel chose to accept the perceived reality that the ten spies' "Grasshopper Report" contained. Fearful of the future challenges that awaited them in the Promised Land, the congregation of Israel murmured, "Why is the LORD bringing us into this land to fall by the sword? Our wives and our little ones will become booty; would it not be better for us to go back to Egypt?" So they said to one another, "Let us choose a captain, and go back to Egypt." Israel's questioning of God is the result of the perception that God had brought them to the present moment for the purpose of "falling by the sword."

Both the response of the ten spies and the response of Israel resulted in fear of the present and future coupled with a desire to cling to the past. We see the fearful result of perceived reality as the congregation of Israel says, "Let us choose a captain, and go back to Egypt." As you will remember, the reality of Egypt was slavery and death, but Israel's fearful perception of reality was far more enslaving and deadly. Guided by its fear of the giants in the Promised Land,

Israel sought the past even though the past held no promise for the future. Controlled by a perceived interpretation of reality, Israel wanted to return to the past because the people knew the reality of life as slaves in Egypt. The biblical word that describes the response of Israel is *murmuring*.

Murmuring is the language of perceived reality. Exodus 15:24 records the first account of murmuring by the people of Israel as they transitioned from the miraculous deliverance of walking on dry ground through the water of the Red Sea and facing the challenges of embarking on a journey through the wilderness to the Promised Land. Three days into their journey, they encountered the reality of non-drinkable, bitter water. Facing this challenge, "the people murmured against Moses."

When the people of Israel encountered the reality of the giants that dwelt in the Promised Land, their first response was also to murmur against Moses. Looking back to Egypt, they told Moses and Aaron, "Would that we had died in the land of Egypt! Or would that we had died in this wilderness! . . . Let us choose a captain, and go back to Egypt." Murmuring is defined by terminology such as "us" and "them" as people make accusations and project blame. Responding to the report of the ten spies, Israel began to speak the murmuring language of perceived reality.

Murmuring is the word that describes life in churches that allow fears of the present and future to be coupled with a desire to cling to the past. In these congregations, murmuring may be heard in church hallways, in Sunday school classes, in parking lots after church meetings, in telephone conversations, and in emails. The topic of murmuring is often disappointment with the perception of a church's present ministry. In murmuring congregations, people often identify the pastor or different church entities as the cause of the problem. "Us," "them," and "you people" color the language in murmuring congregations. Questions in murmuring congregations tend to focus more on fear of the future than hope for the future. In the vocabulary of murmuring, the past tense is heard more often than the future tense. The questions that the murmuring congregation of Israel asked when they received the report of the ten spies may be heard in today's murmuring congregations as follows:

"Why is the LORD bringing us into this land to fall by the sword" could be "Why is the LORD letting us go through this? Our church is going to die."

"Would it not be better for us to go back to Egypt" could be "Wouldn't it be better for us to go back to the old way of doing things?"

"Let us choose a captain, and go back to Egypt" could be "Let us get a new preacher. Let us get a new council chair. Let us organize a new committee so we can be like we were when. . . ."

Whatever the questions or observations may be, the response of murmuring is the same: casting blame in the present by focusing on the past. People live out the behavior pattern of murmuring as they cling to the perceived security of the past even when the past has the power to enslave them in the present.

Envisioned Reality

The interpretation of reality that controlled the response of Joshua and Caleb was Envisioned Reality. Guided by God's promised vision of the future, these two spies challenged the congregation of Israel to trust in God's present and future faithfulness in Numbers 14:7-9 by stating, "The land that we went through as spies is an exceedingly good land. If the LORD is pleased with us, he will bring us into this land and give it to us, a land that flows with milk and honey. Only, do not rebel against the LORD; and do not fear the people of the land, for they are no more than bread for us; their protection is removed from them, and the LORD is with us; do not fear them."

Empowered by their present trust in God's future faithfulness, Joshua and Caleb encouraged the congregation of Israel to face the giants of the Promised Land without fear.

Where the ten spies saw the reality of the Promised Land through their perceived fears of the giants, Joshua and Caleb saw the reality of the Promised Land through the promises of God. Through the frame of this envisioned reality, the focus of these two spies was on God rather than on the giants of the Promised Land. Instead of speaking the vocabulary of murmuring, they spoke the language of "remembering encouragement." Rather than looking to the slavery of the past, they remembered the past faithfulness of God that encouraged them as they lived into the promise of the future. Remembering God's encouraging promise of faith that had been given to Abraham 400 years earlier, they envisioned God's promise for the future. Unlike the ten spies who interpreted the challenges of the present through grasshopper-sized perceptions, Joshua and Caleb interpreted the challenges of the present by a God-sized vision of the future. Remembering God's faithfulness that had led them to the edge of the Promised Land, the focus of their report was on the faithfulness of God instead of our fear of the giants. Speaking the language of present accountability for future possibilities, these two spies spoke the language of trust as they reminded the congregation of Israel that "the LORD is with us."

Today's church can choose to see the challenges of the present through envisioned reality or perceived reality. Our vision and interpretation of reality can allow us to enter God's Promised Land for Jesus' disciples or cause us to wander in the wilderness as we cling to the past. The church's ministry can either be the present fulfillment of God's promises or our ministry can cause wandering in the wilderness of murmuring. To face the present challenges of ministry, a local church must have an understanding of the Promised Land God envisions for disciples of Jesus Christ.

All churches stand on the edge of the Promised Land that Jesus envisioned for his disciples in John 17. All churches face a future they have never traveled with the promise of God's presence. The question a local church must answer as it plans its ministries is the following: will we plan our ministries based on memories of the past, or will we plan ministries formed by the promises of Jesus Christ? The answer to this question will determine whether perceptions of the past or the promise of God's presence guides a church.

There is an important lesson about vision to learn from the account of the spies and the response of the congregation of Israel in the book of Numbers. The lesson is this: both reports regarding the Promised Land were fulfilled. The people who chose to live in the interpretation of reality that the ten spies reported never had the opportunity to enter the Promised Land. They had seen the power and example of God's presence in their exodus from Egypt, but their fear of the challenges in the Promised Land caused them to forget God's promises for the future. Their response to the report of the spies was "'would it not be better for us to go back to Egypt?' and they said to one another, 'Let us choose a captain, and go back to Egypt'" (Numbers 14:3b-4). God offered the people of Israel the freedom of God's promises for the future, but their vision looked to the past because the giants of the Promised Land were in front of them. In their fears, they asked to go back to the days of slavery where at least they knew what was expected of them. Their vision of fear guided them for forty years into a wilderness of death. God's judgment allowed them to live in the reality of their fearful and untrusting vision of life. What was true about God's judgment then is still true today. We experience God's judgment as God allows us to live in the reality of our fearful and untrusting visions of life. What was true about God's grace then is still true today. We experience God's grace as we live with trust in the promises of God's presence and vision for the future.

Disciples of Jesus Christ experience the reality of God's grace as they live with trust in the promise and vision of Jesus' prayer in John 17. The nature of this Promised Land is a church where Jesus' disciples are made complete in his joy, sanctified in the truth of God, and united as Jesus and his "Heavenly Father" are one. Promised Land churches glorify God through their faith as they are called and sent into the world to make God's love known through Jesus. These are communities of faithful disciples who exist to glorify God. Churches that dwell in this Promised Land are expressions of God's grace to a world wandering in the wilderness.

As your congregation considers the Promised Land Jesus envisioned, what vision of reality will you choose?

Praying Together

God of Abraham and God of Moses, through these servants you made known your gift of the Promised Land. We give thanks for the leading of all your faithful servants who point us toward true unity and joy, who point to your Promised Land. As we continue our journey to your Promised Land for Jesus' disciples, guide us to the reality of your promises. We offer this prayer in the name of Jesus who prays for us still, as we continue our journey in faith. Amen.

Seeking God's Vision Together

The following questions provide an opportunity for personal and group reflection as your church seeks God's vision. Te three types of questions will lead you to:

- *Reflect on the scripture passages of the study (Questions for Scriptural Reflection);*
- *Express your opinion regarding the current reality of your church (Helping Your Voice To Be Heard);*
- *Participate in thought and conversation (Questions for Reflection and Discussion).*

Questions for Scriptural Reflection

From the scriptural texts in this chapter, reflect on the following questions and answers:

1. What was the report of the people who were appointed to be visionaries (otherwise known as spies)?

    13:21-29: All of the spies gave the same report regarding the Promised Land. It was a land that flowed with milk and honey. The people who lived in the land were strong, and their towns were fortified.

2. What interpretation of reality did the ten spies report?

    13:31-33: The ten spies reported a perceived interpretation of reality. They gave an unfavorable report saying the people who dwelled in it would defeat them because "to ourselves we seemed like grasshoppers and so we seemed to them."

3. What interpretation of reality did Joshua and Caleb report?

    13:30, 14:7-9: Joshua and Caleb reported an envisioned interpretation of reality. Remembering God's faithfulness in the past, they reminded the congregation of Israel "the Lord is with us; do not fear. . . ."

4. What interpretation of reality did the congregation of Israel choose?

    14:1-4: The congregation of Israel chose a perceived interpretation of reality. A fear of future challenges in the Promised Land caused them to express a desire to return to the slavery of Egypt.

Helping Your Voice To Be Heard

Responses to these questions will formulate information that will allow your church to make intentional decisions about the mission and ministry of your life together. Please enter your responses in the corresponding section of the response sheet provided with this study book. Each answer should be your initial response.

1. I have observed murmuring in our church and have found it to be:
   a. Significantly detrimental;
   b. Somewhat detrimental;

    c. Minimally detrimental;

    d. Not at all detrimental.

2. Does your church have a history of honestly assessing its current reality?

    a. Yes;

    b. No;

    c. Don't know.

3. Issues at your church are decided through:
    a. Envisioned reality;
    b. Perceived reality.

4. Your church's past experience and history:
    a. Hold you back;
    b. Move you forward.

5. Today in our church:
    a. Most people choose to focus on the challenges that are facing our church as the ten spies did;
    b. Most people choose to focus on the promise of God's presence for our church like Joshua and Caleb.

6. Does your church understand that it stands on the edge of God's Promised Land for Jesus' disciples?
    a. Yes;
    b. No;
    c. Don't know.

Questions for Reflection and Discussion

The answers to the following questions provide an opportunity for personal and group reflection as your church seeks God's vision. These will help you know more about your church and each other.

1. Describe a time in your church when there was much "murmuring." How could that issue have been seen from envisioned reality?

2. Why did so many people in the congregation of Israel want to go "back to Egypt"? Discuss what that sounds like in your church.

3. What is the difference between "murmuring" and "remembering encouragement"?

4. Give an example when your church used the language of "remembering encouragement" to claim the promise of God's presence and move forward.

BIBLE STUDY THREE

Overcoming Giants

All Promised Lands have giants dwelling in them: that is the reality of Promised Lands. Some giants are general in nature, and some giants are specific to particular circumstances. If your church wishes to enter the Promised Land Jesus envisioned for his disciples in John 17, what giants does your church need to overcome? What giants do you need to overcome?

Giants in the Promised Land: Numbers 13:25–14:9

If the congregation of Israel was going to live in the Promised Land, they would need to overcome the giants that were dwelling in it. Some of the giants were general in nature; all of the people the spies reported about in the Promised Land were of great size. Some of the giants were specific in nature; the spies' report included people who were known to the congregation of Israel as Nephilim. People of mythic nature, the Nephilim are only mentioned twice in the Old Testament, here in the report of the spies and earlier in Genesis 6:1-3. It is the story of the Nephilim in Genesis 6 that sets the stage for the story of the great flood as they personify the wickedness of humankind. The mere mention of their presence by the spies was enough to cause the congregation of Israel to focus on their self-perceived limitations rather than to live into the vision of God's promise for them.

If a church is going to live in the Promised Land that Jesus envisioned for his faithful disciples, it will also need to overcome giants. Some of these giants are general in nature and face every congregation. Some of the giants are specific to the particular contexts in which congregations may find themselves. These specific giants may have been facing a congregation for generations, or they may have recently developed as a church encounters challenges because of changing demographics, finances, etc.

In order to overcome general and specific giants a congregation must beyond the fearful reality of giants. This will happen only as the congregation focuses on living as people sent into the world through the power of God's love. Blessed by joy and unity, congregations that are able to overcome the giants that face them live as communities of Jesus' disciples who glorify God by their very existence.

This week's study invites you to think about the general giants that face every congregation. The study also invites you to identify the giants that are specific to your congregation. Before we begin our consideration of these giants, let's briefly review how the congregation of Israel responded to the report from the "Promised Land Task Force" and how the context of the congregation of Israel applies to your congregation.

First, the congregation of Israel was standing on the edge of God's promise made to Abraham over 400 years earlier. With the hope of this promise guiding them, God had intervened on behalf of Abraham's descendents to deliver them out of the slavery of Egypt into the hope of a new day.

This same context applies to a local congregation. Every local congregation stands on the edge of God's Promised Land that was envisioned in Jesus' prayer for his disciples almost two thousand years ago. In the hope of this prayer, God intervened on behalf of Jesus' disciples through the life, death, and resurrection of Jesus, delivering them from the slavery of sin and death into this Promised Land of discipleship. In his letter to the Galatians, Paul writes of how God's saving acts through Jesus allow Jesus' followers to participate in the promise of God's faithfulness to Abraham:

> Christ redeemed us from the curse of the law by becoming a curse for us—for it is written, "Cursed is everyone who hangs on a tree"—in order that in Christ Jesus the blessing of Abraham might come to the Gentiles, so that we might receive the promise of the Spirit through faith (Galatians 3:13-14).

> For freedom Christ has set us free. Stand firm, therefore, and do not submit again to a yoke of slavery (Galatians 5:1).

The second context is that members of the congregation of Israel had to choose how they would respond to the general and specific giants that were dwelling in the Promised Land. They had to choose whether they would respond to the challenge of these giants by focusing their vision on the empowering promise of God's faithfulness or by focusing their vision on their self-limiting perceptions of themselves. Their first choice could have empowered them to overcome the giants that were dwelling in the Promised Land. Their second choice left them powerless to respond to the reality of the giants that awaited them.

Local congregations have the same choices to make as they respond to the reality of giants that dwell in God's Promised Land for Jesus' disciples. Members of these congregations may respond to the challenges facing them by focusing their vision on the promise of God's faithfulness. They may also respond to the challenge of the giants by focusing their vision upon themselves. Every congregation must make conscious choices about how it will deal with the general and specific giants it faces.

Some of the general giants facing today's Church are the giant of worldviews, the giant of technology, and the giant of expectation.

The Giant of Worldviews

Society is searching for a bridge that can close the gap between a physical understanding of life and a spiritual understanding of life. While this may seem a modern challenge, this search for understanding is the result of a much longer unfolding of human history. In his book *The Powers That Be,* Walter Wink writes of how the gap between a physical and a spiritual understanding of life has emerged over the span of human existence. Wink offers the observation that this search has occurred through five different worldviews of God and the created order.

The five worldviews that Wink outlines are:

1. The Ancient Worldview: This worldview understood that a spiritual reality mirrored every physical reality. If something happened on earth, a heavenly event mirrored it. If something happened in heaven, an earthly event echoed it. In this worldview, there was a direct connection between the spiritual and the physical. We see an example of this worldview in the story of creation found in Genesis 1:26 when "God said, 'Let us make man in our image, after our likeness.'"

2. The Spiritualist Worldview: In the second century before Christ, a worldview emerged that believed the spirit was good and earthly life was evil. This worldview saw religion's task as rescuing a person's spirit from the flesh and can be seen in Greek philosophy that taught about an eternal soul being held in an earthly shell. With this worldview, however, something significant happened: a separation between the physical and the spiritual occurred in the understanding of human existence.

3. The Materialist Worldview: In what scholars have called the Age of Enlightenment, a worldview emerged that opposed the Spiritualist Worldview. The Materialist Worldview understands human existence as being nothing more than chemicals and atoms that form life. In this worldview, matter is the ultimate force, and the spiritual world is an illusion.

4. The Theological Worldview: In response to a Materialist Worldview, a worldview emerged that conceded earthly reality to science. Theologians, however, claimed that the higher realm of the spirit could not be known by the senses and therefore could not be proven by science. A popular saying that defines this worldview is "Science tells us how the world was created, religion tells us why."

5. The Integral Worldview: A worldview that is emerging in response to all four of these worldviews understands reality in the context of everything having an outer and an inner aspect. Heaven and earth are not seen as mirroring each other. Heaven and earth are seen as the inner and outer aspects of a single reality. There is no separation of spirit and flesh in an Integral Worldview. Instead, there is an integration of spirit and flesh as physical life is defined by an understanding of creation that sees God present in all aspects of life and matter.

As Walter Wink concludes his thoughts on these worldviews, he shares an insight that speaks to people who are searching for a bridge between the physical and the spiritual. Wink writes, "The important point here is that we may be the first generation in the history of the world that can make a conscious choice between these worldviews."[1]

Our modern culture is searching for a sense of direction as we deal with the pressures of life. Within the wilderness of our modern society, people are searching as they struggle with worldviews. They are asking how they can cope with the challenges of life. In the midst of this wilderness, the church is called to make a difference by helping people understand there is a God who cares about them and their world.

The Giant of Technology

Technology is a giant facing the Church in the Promised Land of a new day of ministry. There is no escaping its presence in our homes, in our schools, in our businesses, and in our churches. We live in a society that is rapidly changing and attempting to define itself in the unfolding reality of technology.

As has always been the case, the technology of the society in which we live will determine methods and tools by which we may communicate the Good News. It is important to realize, however, that society does not define the message of Jesus Christ. That message is the same yesterday, today, and forever (Hebrews 13:8). It is also essential to realize this eternal message presents the church with the possibility for reaching people at a level of interaction that technology alone is unable to achieve: the need to be connected to God's sacred touch.

The story of God's sacred touch upon human life is the story of the Bible. Genesis 2:7 tells of how "the LORD God formed man from the dust of the ground, and breathed into his nostrils the breath of life; and the man became a living being." Genesis 3 tells the repeating story of how humanity chooses to live outside of a trusting relationship with God, who breathes life into our very existence. From this original sin emerges the remaining story of the Bible. It is the story of a God continually reaching out to a creation that has fallen from God's spoken goodness, a creation whose image is blurred by mistrust and willful self-interests. It is the story of God's Word becoming flesh and dwelling among humanity "full of grace and truth" (John 1:14). Ultimately, it is the redemptive story of God's sacred touch being restored to humankind through a new heaven and a new earth as God wipes "every tear from their eyes" (Revelation 21:4).

The story of God's sacred touch gives the church the power and authority to speak to a meaning of life that is beyond human knowledge.

In the summer 1995 issue of *Inc. Technology,* there is a brief report from Don DeLillo of a "Talk of the Nation" interview with Ray Suarez:

> (Technology) knows everything about us. And it causes a level of anxiety that is sort of quietly pervasive. . . . In the technology of industry, we worry about the damage to the environment. In the technology of weapons, we're concerned about their potential for destruction. In the technology of nuclear energy, we sometimes find ourselves a little worried about what will happen if there's an accident. So there's something beneath the domestic veneer of our lives that is carried somewhat perniciously by the force of technology. And it causes an odd sort of almost unrealizable dread. . . . Every generation has a new sense of the sophistication of the technology being developed and how it will solve . . . certain problems of perception, how it will be superior to what we've had before. But sometimes it just doesn't. There are some difficulties, there are human anxieties, that can't be satisfied by the most sophisticated technology. [2]

The church speaks the language of trust as it offers a message of hope that the giant of technology cannot satisfy. Providing the assurance of God's presence, the ministry of the church can meet people in the deepest concerns of their lives.

The Giant of Expectation

Advances in technology create the expectation that life will become more meaningful and relevant. Much fanfare awaited the arrival of the iPhone in the summer of 2007 as people waited in lines overnight to be the first to own this new product of technology. Roger Entner, of market-research firm IAG, spoke about the expectations associated with Apple's new cell phone debut on June 29, 2007:

> It's a product of mythical proportions. They're not saying the iPhone will . . . bring world peace, but that it will do everything else. It's impossible to live up to these expectations. [3]

The giant of expectation, however, is not only seen in technology. People have expectations by which they measure relevancy as they value meaning and worth for their lives. There are generational expectations, institutional expectations, and theological expectations that can cause conflict to rise within a church as persons search for meaning. It is at the convergence and divergence of expectations that the church has the holy responsibility of helping persons understand their meaning and worth through the eternal story of God's love in Jesus Christ. This is where the giant of expectation affects the ministry of a local church. If persons perceive the ministry of a local church as being less than relevant to their present concerns and expectations of life, then they will dismiss that church as being irrelevant. The good news is that people can also understand a local church as being relevant. This will happen as that church helps them to envision a life that is beyond their expectations. To accept this challenge, a congregation must equip itself for a new day of ministry as it connects persons with the eternal message of God's love in ways that are relevant to the present challenges of life.

Within the wilderness of our modern society, people are searching for meaning. They are struggling with worldviews and gigantic expectations. They are struggling with their own giants. In the midst of this struggle, the church is called to connect people to the sacred touch of a God who can wipe away every tear as they enter the Promised Land of God's love and of meaning for their lives.

Giants Facing Your Local Congregation

In addition to the general giants that face the church, every local church has specific giants that it faces in the context of its ministry setting. Some of these giants may be a congregation with a history of conflict, a congregation that limits its leadership base to a few selected members who maintain or exchange the same offices within the church, a congregation that does not reflect the diversity of its changing neighborhood, a congregation with an aging facility, a congregation of limited resources, etc. Over time, specific giants can take on mythical proportions as they shape and control the culture and structure of a congregation. When allowed, specific giants can cause members to focus on their own concerns of institutional survival rather than to looking beyond themselves for missional expressions of God's Holy Spirit. Instead of living as people who envision God's promise of faithfulness for Jesus' disciples, limiting self-perceptions control these congregations.

The story of Israel's response to the report of the ten spies in Numbers 13:30–14:9 is the story of every congregation that is controlled by self-perceptions rather than by God's promise of faithfulness. Faced with the choice of focusing beyond the giants through the promise of God's faithfulness or focusing within themselves, the congregation of Israel chose the latter. In the process, the culture of their congregation changed from hopeful possibility to fear. Another manifestation of their inward focus was the attempt to change their structure as they wanted to elect a captain to lead them back to Egypt. Rather than focusing beyond themselves, they focused on their survival as they faced the giants in the Promised Land.

When a congregation structures its ministry upon its survival as the reason for its existence, it will wander in search of meaning. The culture of this congregation will focus on the preservation of the institution rather than its mission. Structures will be put in place that result in repeated ministry patterns that either protect cherished memories of the past or guard cherished ministries of the present. Congregations that focus within their own self-perceptions will experience weariness and murmuring as ministry efforts keep yielding the same results. At some point, talk will begin to surface among members about the future viability of the church as worship attendance plateaus and declines and resources become limited. Rather than focusing beyond themselves, these congregations focus on their survival as they face the giants that dwell in the Promised Land.

If a church is going to overcome these giants, it must allow its culture to be affected by the promise of God's faithfulness. It must make intentional choices that will allow it to structure itself to see beyond the giants and comprehend future possibilities for ministry that God will empower. This is not an easy process. It requires courage to speak the truth in love as people ask the right questions, align vision and mission with structures for ministry, and focus the culture of the congregation on the self-giving love of Jesus. As a congregation lives into a model for mission that focuses beyond itself as the reason for its existence, it will be able to overcome the giants that are facing it.

Wandering in the wilderness or overcoming giants, what choice do you make?

Praying Together

> God of all creation, giver of life, through the ages your sustenance and strength have kept your people. You never abandon us; you are always at our side; you are closer than our very breath. We thank you for your presence as we journey through the challenges of life. We thank you that you are able to redeem our fears, our poor choices, and our missed opportunities, making them strong for your purposes. As we continue our journey to your Promised Land for Jesus' disciples, remind us that you go before us ushering in your kingdom. In the strong name of Jesus we pray. Amen.

Seeking God's Vision Together

The following questions provide an opportunity for personal and group reflection as your church seeks God's vision. The three types of questions will lead you to:

- *Reflect on the scripture passages of the study (Questions for Scriptural Reflection);*
- *Express your opinion regarding the current reality of your church (Helping Your Voice To Be Heard);*
- *Participate in thought and conversation (Questions for Reflection and Discussion).*

Questions for Scriptural Reflection

From the scriptural texts in this chapter, reflect on the following questions and answers:

1. Why was the congregation of Israel unable to enter the Promised Land?

   Numbers 14:2-3: They focused on the challenges facing them rather than on the promise God had made to Abraham.

   Numbers 14:4: They desired to return to the past.

2. Why was the congregation of Israel powerless to respond to the challenges of the future?

Numbers 14:9: They allowed their fears to control them.

3. Why do local congregations stand on the edge of God's Promised Land?

Galatians 3:13-14: God's promise of faithfulness and f the blessing of Abraham have been fulfilled through Jesus.

Helping Your Voice To Be Heard

Responses to these questions will formulate information that will allow your church to make intentional decisions about the mission and ministry of your life together. Please enter your responses in the corresponding section of the response sheet provided with this study book. Each answer should be your initial response.

1. Can your church name the giants that are preventing you from entering God's Promised Land of joy and unity?
   a. Yes;
   b. No.

2. Does your church focus more on the giants that are facing it than on God's vision for the future?
   a. Focus more on the giants;
   b. Focus more on God's vision for the future.

3. Has your church demonstrated the courage to make intentional choices that will empower it to overcome the giants that are facing it?
   a. Yes;
   b. No.

4. Would your community consider your church to be relevant to the present challenges of life?
   a. Yes;
   b. No;
   c. Don't know.

5. What are the current giants that are facing your church? (Choose up to three.)
   a. Lack of age diversity in the congregation;
   b. A changing neighborhood;
   c. Financial challenges;
   d. Aging facility;
   e. Changes in the number of church members;
   f. Worship attendance;
   g. History of conflict;

    h. Other.

6. What are strengths within your congregation that can help your church to overcome the giants it faces?
    a. Worship;
    b. Location;
    c. Spiritual formation opportunities;
    d. Mission;
    e. Church facility;
    f. Financial strength;
    g. Communication.

Questions for Reflection and Discussion

The answers to the following questions provide an opportunity for personal and group reflection as your church seeks God's vision. These questions will help you know more about your church and each other.

1. How would you describe the Promised Land of joy and unity that God has placed before your congregation?

2. Discuss the impact of the general giants of Worldviews, Technology, and Expectation upon the life of your church.

3. What specific giants are unique to your church?
    a. Do any of these specific giants have a history in your church that causes great fear?
    b. What is the greatest giant that is causing your church to live in fear of the future?

3. How are these specific giants preventing your congregation from entering the Promised Land of joy and unity for Jesus' disciples?

4. Describe a time when your church overcame a giant it faced.

5. How might your church respond to the challenges that are before it?

End Notes

1. Walter Wink, *The Powers That Be, Theology for a New Millennium* (New York: Galilee Doubleday,1999)15-22.
2. "Tech Noise," in *Inc. Technology,* Summer 1995, 18.
3. "Perspectives" in *Newsweek*, July 2/July9, 2008, 25.

Asking the Right Questions

Where do we find true power? The Gospel of Mark invites you to ask the right questions as you walk on the path of discipleship that leads to the cross and empty tomb of Jesus. On this path, you must answer questions that Jesus asks all of his disciples: questions such as "What were you discussing on the way?" and "Who do you say that I am?" Your answers to these questions will say much about where you find true power in your life and in the life of your church.

"What were you discussing on the way?" Mark 9:30-35 records this question of Jesus. The setting for this question is Galilee, where Jesus first called his disciples to follow him so that they could become fishers of people.

A Discussion along the Way: Mark 9:30-35

It is no accident that Jesus chose Galilee as the location to teach his disciples about true power he taught them about his impending crucifixion and resurrection. There are three instances in the Gospel of Mark where Galilee is the site of powerful lessons about discipleship. The first is in Mark 1:14-20 where Jesus initially called his disciples to follow as he invites them to become fishers of people. The second is recorded in Mark 9:30-35 as Jesus instructs his disciples about his impending crucifixion and resurrection. The third invitation to understand the lesson of discipleship is recorded in Mark 16:6-7 when a messenger from God delivers an invitation for the disciples to return to Galilee where they will meet the risen Christ, who is going before them. Throughout Mark, Galilee is a crucial turning point in the path of discipleship. Galilee is where Jesus invites the disciples to follow him in his earthly ministry, his crucifixion, and his resurrection. It is where they begin to understand where true power is found.

Immediately after Jesus teaches about his crucifixion and resurrection, he takes his disciples from Galilee to Capernaum. Here Jesus continues the lesson he has begun about true power by asking the right question of the disciples: "What were you arguing about on the way?" This question may also be translated as "What were you discussing on the way?" Regardless of the translation, the context for this question by Jesus is that the disciples have been debating on the way: "Who is the greatest among us?"

Jesus could have taught the disciples a lesson about greatness by letting them know who was really the greatest among them. He could have yielded to the temptation of attempting to control the disciples' power struggle. Instead, Jesus asked the right question as he confronted them regarding their conflict: "What were you discussing on the way?" Jesus' question left the disciples speechless as they struggled with the reality of their desire for control. Responding to their power struggle, Jesus invited the twelve disciples to gather in community as he sat with them and taught them where true power is found: "Whoever wants to be first must be last of all and servant of all."

We can learn a lot about a person's intent from the questions he or she asks. The Gospel of Mark records forty-seven instances where Jesus asks questions. In addition to these questions by Jesus, Mark also records twelve accounts of questions asked by religious leaders, seven questions asked by the crowds and individuals, five questions asked by Pilate, and two questions by unclean spirits. In Mark, there are questions of faith and faithlessness, questions intended to clarify and muddy the waters, questions of life and death, and questions of hope and despair. There are questions intended to control Jesus and questions that define the life, crucifixion, and resurrection of Jesus Christ as the Good News is proclaimed. In the end, all of the questions lead to one point: where is true power found?

Where do you find true power? Where does your church find true power? To arrive at the answer to these questions, it is essential to consider the first and last questions recorded in Mark as well as the questions Jesus asks all of his disciples: "What were you discussing on the way?" and "Who do you say that I am?" As you consider these questions, reflect on the questions you are hearing in your community of faith. At the conclusion of this study, you will be invited to consider the right questions your church should be asking.

The first question in Mark is drastically different from the initial searching questions of the other gospels. The Magi ask the first question in Matthew in response to a sign of the Messiah's birth: "Where is the child who has been born king of the Jews?" Zechariah asks the first question in Luke in response to an angelic message regarding the birth of John the Baptist: "How will I know that this is so?" Religious leaders ask the first question in John when they inquire of John the Baptist, "Who are you?"

An unclean spirit asks the initial question in Mark (1:23). This question follows Jesus' first teaching session in Capernaum (the same location where Jesus is now teaching his disciples about true power). The setting for this teaching moment is Sabbath worship in the synagogue.

After the synagogue worshipers have acknowledged the authority of Jesus in Mark 1:22, a man with an unclean spirit interrupts Jesus' teaching moment. Confronting Jesus, the spirit asks, "What have you to do with us, Jesus of Nazareth? Have you come to destroy us?" (Mark 1:23). The confrontation does not conclude with these questions, as the unclean spirit states, "I know who you are, the Holy One of God." At first hearing, it may seem that the unclean spirit is simply identifying who Jesus is. After all, the unclean spirit correctly names Jesus as the Holy One of God. There is far more at stake in this account. Rather than simply stating Jesus' identity, the unclean spirit is attempting to engage Jesus in a power struggle that would limit Jesus' identity. Jesus would not allow the destructive questions of the unclean spirit to limit his identity. The Holy One of God was not going to allow the wrong questions to define his ministry. Jesus' ministry was about redemption rather than destruction. Rather than allowing himself to become involved in a power struggle with the unclean spirit, Jesus commanded the spirit to "be silent and come out of him" (Mark 1:25).

Power struggles are not simple matters. When we engage in power struggles, we attempt to limit the identity and power of other people. Rather than building community, power struggles destroy relationships as we define sides by "us" and "them." In power struggles, questions about the true motives of other people fly about: "What do you really want? Why are you trying to change us?" Accusations such as "I know what you're trying to do. You don't care about _____. All you care about is _____" soon follow as we attempt to exert control. Labels such as *conservative*, *liberal*, *fundamentalist*, or *non-biblical* are designed to discredit people with whom we disagree as we attempt to limit their power upon our lives. If we are not mindful, we can become possessed by the questions we ask, the accusations we make, and the labels we project when we engage in power struggles. It is ironic to note that worship provided the context for the first power struggle of Jesus' ministry recorded in the Gospel of Mark. It is equally ironic to note that worship continues to provide the context for power struggles in the ministry of many of today's churches. Adding a new service of worship or changing the tradition of a present service of worship can cause tension within the life of a church. In the presence of this tension, right questions can lead to conflict resolution and stronger community life, or wrong questions can lead to the destruction of relationships.

When people or churches experience tension or conflict, it is essential to understand the context in which questions are asked. Right questions invite dialogue, understanding, and strengthening of community and relationship. Wrong questions invite accusation, labeling, and destruction of community and relationship. Worship is not the only ministry where the church experiences tension. Decisions about church leadership, ministries, finances, and personnel can also be sources of conflict within the life of a church.

People of faith in Jesus Christ must listen carefully and understand the questions we are asking as well as the questions other people are asking when we find ourselves in the midst of conflict. We must listen carefully and understand the questions we are asking because our *intent* resides in our questions. Do our questions and the questions of other people invite dialogue, understanding, and strengthening of community, or do our questions and the questions of other people invite accusation, labeling, and destruction of community? Do our questions define our identity through our faith in the Holy One of God, or do our questions allow us to become possessed by power struggles?

Jesus would not allow himself to become possessed by the questions the unclean spirit asked. When necessary, do we respond to power struggles by making a public statement that we are not going to allow ourselves to be controlled by the questions that are being asked? Jesus would not allow his disciples to ask the wrong questions as they argued among themselves about who was the greatest in God's kingdom. Jesus redirected their questions by asking the right question: "What were you discussing on the way?" Following this question, Jesus then invited his disciples to engage in community as he taught them that true power resides in being last of all and servant of all. When appropriate, do we respond to power struggles by asking questions that redirect conflict to the true power of being last of all and servant of all?

In Mark, Jesus defined the power of his identity as the Holy One of God by refusing to allow the wrong questions to possess him and by asking the right questions that identified him as the servant of all and last of all. Another question that defined Jesus' identity is recorded in Mark 8:29. Jesus is with his disciples at Caesarea Philippi, a site of pagan worship and a symbol of earthly Roman power, when he asks, "Who do you say that I am?" It is a vulnerable moment for Jesus, and the first time in the Gospel of Mark that he gives his disciples the power to state his identity. On behalf of the disciples, Peter answers, "You are the Christ." Immediately after Peter correctly identifies Jesus as the Christ, Mark 8:31-35 records Jesus defining the call of discipleship through the reality of the cross with these words:

> Then he began to teach them that the Son of Man must undergo great suffering, and be rejected by the elders, the chief priests, and the scribes, and be killed, and after three days rise again. He said all this quite openly. And Peter took him aside and began to rebuke him. But turning and looking at his disciples, he rebuked Peter and said, "Get behind me, Satan! For you are setting your mind not on divine things but on human things." He called the crowd with his disciples, and said to them, "If any want to become my followers, let them deny themselves and take up their cross and follow me. For those who want to save their life will lose it, and those who lose their life for my sake, and for the sake of the gospel, will save it."

In reading this scripture, it is important to note the power struggle that occurs between Jesus and Peter as Jesus plainly redefines the calling of discipleship from being fishers of people to being cross bearers. Following this redefining of the ministry of discipleship, Peter (who correctly identified Jesus as the Christ) openly confronts Jesus by rebuking him. Although Peter's rebuke of Jesus may seem to be an innocent statement of concern for Jesus' safety, Peter is actually attempting to control Jesus' identity as the Christ. Rather than accepting Jesus' teaching about crucifixion and resurrection, Peter is attempting to define and confine Jesus by his own understanding of power. Peter is much more comfortable with a Christ who is a fisher of people than he is with a Christ who invites him to walk the path to Calvary.

Following Peter's rebuke, Jesus turns, sees his disciples, and rebukes Peter. To understand the full impact of Jesus' rebuke of Peter, it is important to note that the Greek word for rebuke, *epitimao*, is used only twice in Mark. One instance is here in Mark 8:31-35 where Jesus rebukes Peter as Peter attempts to limit Jesus' identity as the Christ. The other instance is found in Mark 1:25 where Jesus rebukes the unclean spirit as the spirit attempts to limit Jesus' identity as the Holy One of God. On both occasions, Jesus would not allow such attempts to limit his identity.

When power struggles confront disciples of Jesus Christ, we need to be mindful of where true power resides as we define our identities and our ministries through Jesus' calling upon our lives. One of the sad realities churches face is that people or groups would rather watch a congregation become less effective in ministry, decline, and sometimes die because they do not want to give up their power. Groups within these congregations define themselves through the terminology of "us" and "them" as one group or faction seeks to dominate another. In describing congregations that are engaged in power struggles, people will sometimes say that a church may have to die before resurrection can occur. While this observation may sound right, it stands against Jesus' teaching about true power as Jesus' disciples become the last of all and servant of all. Jesus did not teach that true power is found through death. Jesus taught that true power is found through the cross. As Jesus taught his disciples about the cross, he was teaching them about the reality of power in God's kingdom. Jesus told them that if they were to follow him they must deny themselves, take up their crosses, and follow him on the path that leads to Calvary. Remember that the journey of Christian discipleship leads to the cross of the crucified Jesus Christ before it leads to the empty tomb of the resurrected Jesus Christ.

Anyone can die. Not everyone can submit to God's definition of power by denying self and following Jesus through the power of the cross. Any church can die. Not every church can submit to God's definition of power and allow past and present power struggles to be crucified as that church lives into an identity defined by the reality of the cross of Jesus Christ.

Power struggles can possess a church throughout its history. Names and identities of people may change, but the power struggles remain the same as history repeats itself through a changing cast. Churches become involved in a repetition of power struggles because leaders and members may find themselves fearful of asking the right questions that will lead to a resurrected understanding of where they will find true power. The joyful unity that Jesus envisioned for his disciples in his prayer of John 17 is a rare occurrence in these congregations. Perhaps the biblical reference that best describes life in these congregations is from 1 Samuel 3:1: "The word of the LORD was rare in those days; visions were not widespread."

When power struggles possess a church, the leaders and members of that church must ask themselves if they are willing to engage in a new way of thinking as they say who they think Jesus is. Instead of speaking about "winners" or "losers," will the congregation begin to speak about what it means to be "last of all and servant of all"? Instead of making statements about who is right and who is wrong, will the congregation begin to ask questions about where it will find God's true power when its members confess Jesus as Christ? When congregations are willing to die as they struggle with the world's definition of power rather than living in the power of the cross, the question the church needs to ask is if they are willing to let go of their power struggles for Jesus' sake and the gospel's. The cross of Jesus Christ asks every congregation what it values most as that congregation answers the question Jesus asks of all his followers, "Who do you say that I am?"

Mary Magdalene, Mary the mother of James, and Salome ask the last question recorded in Mark when they go to the tomb early on the first day of the week to anoint the crucified Jesus: "Who will roll away the stone for us from the entrance to the tomb?" (Mark 16:3). Following this question, Mark 16:4-7 states the following:

> When they looked up, they saw that the stone, which was very large, had already been rolled back. As they entered the tomb, they saw a young man, dressed in a white robe, sitting on the right side; and they were alarmed. But he said to them, "Do not be alarmed; you are looking for Jesus of Nazareth, who was crucified. He has been raised; he is not here. Look, there is the place they laid him. But go, tell his disciples and Peter that he is going ahead of you to Galilee; there you will see him, just as he told you."

There is a powerful difference between the first question recorded in Mark and the last question recorded in Mark. The first question by the unclean spirit is an attempt to confine the power of the Holy One of God. The last question asked on Easter morning opens our lives to the reality of the empty tomb and the power of the Holy One of God. At times this reality is frighteningly astonishing because Jesus' disciples are invited to live in a new understanding of power: the Easter power of the crucified and resurrected Jesus Christ. Easter is Jesus' invitation to live in the victory of Calvary. Easter is Jesus' invitation to follow him as the risen Christ by living a life that has a future.

How many times have you heard people or churches wonder if they have a future? This question is often couched in discussions of past power struggles that have reproduced themselves into present power struggles. The good news of the empty tomb is that God offers followers of Jesus resurrected possibilities of life through a future they have not yet experienced. It is a powerful invitation, a frightening invitation, an invitation to take up the cross and live by losing their lives for the sake of Jesus and the gospel.

All of this leads to the question that began this Bible study: "What were you discussing on the way?" It is the question that Jesus asked of his disciples when they were engaged in a power struggle over who was the greatest among them. It is the question that leaders and members of congregations need to answer as they accept Jesus' invitation to live in the victory of Calvary and follow him as the risen Christ by living a life that has a future. This right question will extend an invitation for dialogue to communities of faith just as it extended an invitation for dialogue to Jesus and the disciples. This right question will open the door to conversation about greatness and power in God's kingdom. It will allow disciples of Jesus to define their identity and their ministry as they seek to be last of all and servants of all. Perhaps this question will allow congregations and people entombed by power struggles of the past and present to look up and see that the stone has been rolled away.

Are you asking the right question? What questions are you hearing in your church and in your life?

Praying Together

> God of all power and might, you have made us in your image. We rejoice in this very thought. But as we seek your face, we tend to define power from a worldly perspective that distorts your perfect power of grace. As we continue our journey to your Promised Land for Jesus' disciples, give us the wisdom and courage to submit to your definition of power and to embrace your call to serve in your name. In the name of the one whose resurrection power leads us, we pray. Amen.

Seeking God's Vision Together

The following questions provide an opportunity for personal and group reflection as your church seeks God's vision. The three types of questions will lead you to:

- *Reflect on the scripture passages of the study (Questions for Scriptural Reflection);*
- *Express your opinion regarding the current reality of your church (Helping Your Voice To Be Heard);*
- *Participate in thought and conversation (Questions for Reflection and Discussion).*

Questions for Scriptural Reflection

From the scriptural texts in this chapter, reflect on the following questions and answers:

1. What happened when Jesus asked the right question, "What were you discussing on the way?"

   Mark 9:33-35: Jesus' question allowed the disciples to stop focusing on their power struggle about who was the greatest among them.

   Jesus' question allowed him to begin teaching the disciples that true power is found when his followers are the last of all and the servant of all.

2. What happened when Jesus asked the right question, "Who do you say that I am?"

   Mark 8:31-35: Jesus' question allowed him to define his own identity as the Christ.

3. What happened when Jesus asked the right question, "My God, my God, why have you forsaken me?"

Mark 15:34-39: By becoming the least and the last on the cross, Jesus' true identity as the Holy One of God was revealed.

4. Why didn't the disciples ask Jesus questions about his teaching regarding his impending crucifixion?

Mark 9:30-32: They were afraid to ask Jesus questions because they did not understand the true power about which Jesus taught.

5. What happened when Mary Magdalene, Mary the mother of James, and Salome asked the right question, "Who will roll away the stone for us from the door of the tomb?"

Mark 16:3-8: They heard the Easter message about the true power of the crucified and risen Christ.

Helping Your Voice To Be Heard

Responses to these questions will formulate information that will allow your church to make intentional decisions about the mission and ministry of your life together. Please enter your responses in the corresponding section of the response sheet provided with this study book. Each answer should be your initial response.

1. Would you say that "hallway conversations" at your church are usually meant to:
   a. Gain understanding;
   b. Complain;
   c. Resolve conflict;
   d. Accuse and blame.

2. Do questions in your church have a tendency to:
   a. Build community;
   b. Destroy relationships.

3. Jesus asked his disciples, "What were you discussing on the way?" What does your church spend time discussing? (Pick four.)
   a. Present ministries;
   b. The past;
   c. Future ministries;
   d. Who Jesus is;
   e. Who's right or who's wrong;
   f. Spreading the Good News;
   g. What happened on Sunday;
   h. Finances;
   i. Lay leadership;
   j. Staff leadership;
   k. Concerns of your church;
   l. Concerns of your community;
   m. Defining your church's mission;
   n. Long-term survival;
   o. Disappointing ministries;
   p. Successful ministries;
   q. How to get more people involved;
   r. Worship attendance.

4. What labels have you heard used in your church? (Pick three.)
   a. Those new members;   e. Involved;
   b. Those old timers;   f. Uninvolved;
   c. Us;   g. Committed;
   d. Them;   h. Not committed.

5. Does your congregation focus on?
   a. Power struggles;
   b. Ministry.

6. Does your church have questions about its future?
   a. Yes;
   b. No;
   c. Don't know.

7. Do questions in your church invite dialogue from diverse opinions?
   a. Yes;
   b. No;
   c. Don't know.

8. Does the history of your church reflect power struggles that it continues to repeat?
   a. Yes;
   b. No;
   c. Don't know.

9. Is there agreement or disagreement about what your congregation values most?
   a. Agreement;
   b. Disagreement;
   c. Don't know.

Questions for Reflection and Discussion

The answers to the following questions provide an opportunity for personal and group reflection as your church seeks God's vision. These questions will help you know more about your church and each other.

1. Where does power reside in your church?

2. What appears to be limiting your church's ministry?

3. Tell about a time when a person or group of people in your church modeled Jesus' leadership by being last of all and servant of all.

Beyond and Within

Jesus' disciples were facing an identity crisis. The reality of discipleship was changing. The reality of Jesus' first invitation to discipleship made sense as he called them to be fishers of people. Mark 1:16-20 records that Jesus' first invitation to discipleship made such perfect sense to Simon, Andrew, James, and John that they immediately began to follow him:

> As Jesus passed along the Sea of Galilee, he saw Simon and his brother Andrew casting a net into the sea—for they were fishermen. And Jesus said to them, "Follow me and I will make you fish for people." And immediately they left their nets and followed him. As he went a little farther, he saw James son of Zebedee and his brother John, who were in their boat mending the nets. Immediately he called them; and they left their father Zebedee in the boat with the hired men, and followed him.

Simon, Andrew, James, and John could identify with the reality of being fishers of people. They understood the wisdom of this invitation to discipleship. Their lives had prepared them for this invitation by Jesus. Along the way of this fishing trip, however, the waters began to get choppy. There were people who welcomed Jesus with open arms as the nets of his ministry gathered them into the good news of God's kingdom. There were also people who did not appreciate the nets Jesus was casting for God's kingdom. In fact, they grew to despise Jesus because he challenged the reality of their identity as religious leaders.

Jesus could tell that the rough water he was encountering was a prelude to a perfect storm as he issued a second invitation to discipleship in Mark 8:34-37:

> He called the crowd with his disciples, and said to them, "If any want to become my followers, let them deny themselves and take up their cross and follow me. For those who want to save their life will lose it, and those who lose their life for my sake, and for the sake of the gospel, will save it. For what will it profit them to gain the whole world and forfeit their life? Indeed, what can they give in return for their life?"

Assessing current reality, Jesus could tell that the cost of following him on the path of discipleship was going to require his disciples to live in a new reality. In assessing current reality, it is essential to note that the call to discipleship remained the same in Mark 8:34-37 as it did in Mark 1:14-20: following Jesus. It is also essential to note that while the essence of Jesus' call to discipleship remained the same, the reality of discipleship changed drastically. It is one thing to leave your nets behind as you fish for bigger fish with Jesus. It is another thing to take up your cross and lose your life for Jesus' sake and for the gospel's on the path to discipleship.

Jesus' second invitation to discipleship was a call to a journey that was beyond the past and present context of his disciples' lives. Up to that point, Jesus' first invitation to discipleship had led to success that was beyond the world's wisdom: the sick had been healed, unclean spirits had been driven out of people's lives, the kingdom of God had been revealed through the preaching and teaching of Jesus, new life had been given to the dead, the hungry had been fed, Jesus had walked on water. Jesus could tell, however, that the past and present successes of his first invitation to discipleship were not going to reveal the full extent of God's kingdom. There was only one way that could be done: Calvary. Assessing the current reality of his ministry, Jesus extended a second invitation to discipleship that envisioned a life that was beyond his disciples' current understanding of reality. A biblical principle called *Beyond and Within* defines this second invitation to discipleship.

Beyond and Within teaches that the current reality of discipleship is assessed through the transforming truth of the cross of Jesus. This invitation to discipleship mandates that the vision of discipleship must be beyond self-focused concerns as Jesus' followers take up their cross and lose their lives for Jesus' sake and the gospel's. Faithful acceptance of this invitation results in transformation through intentional choices that define the vision and values of life.

Just as is true for an individual disciple's life, communities of Jesus' disciples must live by the principle of *Beyond and Within* if they wish to be transformed. Congregations that live by the biblical principle of *Beyond and Within* realize that if they want to live in the vision of the risen Christ, they must first look to the cross of the crucified Christ. The goal for ministry within these congregations is that people may be nurtured and equipped to live as Jesus' disciples as the present values of their lives are transformed.

Beyond and Within is a scriptural foundation for churches that seek to share the love of God through an outward focus. Churches that apply this biblical teaching assess the current reality of their ministry by how they are nurturing people to be disciples of Jesus as they are equipped to see beyond their self-focused concerns. Remembering Jesus' admonition about losing life for his sake and the gospel's, they share the love of God by focusing beyond their own concerns.

Through this same self-giving vision, they also look within at those things that are hindering them from living as God's called people. Following Jesus' sacrificial example of love, the cross of Jesus transforms them. They have accepted Jesus' second invitation to discipleship even though it means they may have to face an identity crisis as they assess the current reality of their ministries.

Congregations transformed by the biblical principle of Jesus' second invitation to discipleship understand that the resurrection of a new day for ministry is possible only through the cross of Jesus Christ. They understand that an honest assessment of the present reality of ministry may require a new vision that is beyond all that has led to their past or present successes. Rather than protecting cherished memories of the past or cherished ministries of the present, they focus their concerns on how they may share the gospel of Jesus Christ in the present reality of their ministry. Answering Jesus' transformational call to follow, they understand that the journey of discipleship is always a journey beyond the past and present context of their church's life.

It is easy for a church to seek to save its life. Cherished memories of holy moments that should be the foundation for empowering a church's future ministry can easily become chains that hinder a congregation from living into the future. The challenges of ministry facing a church as it anticipates the giants that dwell in God's Promised Land can cause some congregations to look within themselves rather than beyond themselves. Instead of being identified by the joy and unity for which Jesus prayed, some congregations are defined by the tension of strife and dissension. Rather than glorifying God by living as Jesus' sent people, some churches wander in the wilderness as they search for a reason for their existence or live in the emptiness of self-focus.

Two portions of scripture that speak to the reason for the church's existence are the Great Commission of Matthew 28:16-20 and the Great Promise of Acts 1:8.

Jesus gives the Great Commission of Matthew 28:16-20 at Galilee where he began his ministry. This home base for Jesus' earthly ministry becomes the launching point for his resurrected ministry as he commissions his disciples to answer a world-changing calling:

> Now the eleven disciples went to Galilee, to the mountain to which Jesus had directed them. When they saw him, they worshiped him; but some doubted. And Jesus came and said to them, "All authority in heaven and on earth has been given to me. Go therefore and make disciples of all nations, baptizing them in the name of the Father and of the Son and of the Holy Spirit, and teaching them to obey everything that I have commanded you. And remember, I am with you always, to the end of the age."

Jesus gives the Great Promise of Acts 1:8 at Bethany. Bethany was the village that served as the beginning point for Jesus' Palm Sunday entrance into Jerusalem. Riding on a donkey into the Holy City, Jesus taught about true power as he answered the call of being last of all

and servant of all. It is at Bethany that the resurrected Jesus promises the power of God's kingdom to his disciples:

> "But you will receive power when the Holy Spirit has come upon you; and you will
> be my witnesses in Jerusalem, in all Judea and Samaria, and to the ends of the earth."

In both the Great Commission and the Great Promise, the envisioned reality of Jesus' disciples being called to a life of faith in a crucified and risen Lord defines the existence of the church.
The Great Commission teaches that the purpose of worship, teaching, and remembering is to
strengthen the church's witness of focusing beyond itself as it goes and makes "disciples of all
nations, baptizing them in the name of the Father and of the Son and of the Holy Spirit." The
Great Promise teaches that the purpose of power from the Holy Spirit is for Jesus' disciples to
be his "witnesses in Jerusalem and in all Judea and Samaria and to the ends of the earth." This
calling empowers congregations of Jesus' disciples to focus beyond themselves as they accept
Jesus' invitation to take up their cross and follow their Savior in sacrificial living. Through an outward focus for ministry, these congregations offer encouragement and hope for the future as
they connect with people who are looking for help to face the giants within their lives.

Churches that allow their own needs to become the primary concern for their existence
live in a different reality. Reversing the order of the biblical principle of *Beyond and Within* to
"Within and Beyond," these congregations see with grasshopper-sized vision as they allow their
self-confining concerns to become the focus of their existence. Instead of allowing their ministry to look beyond their own needs, they seek to save their own lives. Looking within they
have little, if any, outward connection with their communities. Cherished memories can chain
these churches to the past. They face the challenges of the present by wandering in discouragement as they dwell on their past memories of success rather than envisioning possibilities of
hope for their future. Current cherished ministries can chain these churches to the present and
focus their energy on maintaining the comfort level within the congregation rather than allowing the congregation to look beyond. Whatever the reason, if an inward focus defines the existence of a church, that congregation will become a symbol of irrelevance as it attempts to
communicate God's message of grace through Jesus Christ with society. If a church's goal for
ministry is to maintain its current successes or replicate past successes, it will wander in the
wilderness of searching for a reason for its future existence.

In order for a congregation to enter God's Promised Land for Jesus' disciples, its members
must be willing to honestly assess if the needs of their congregation are causing them to focus
within themselves rather than beyond themselves. Acts 6:1-7 is an example of a congregation
that honestly assessed its current reality. The congregation in this scripture was the first
Christian congregation in Jerusalem. Membership within the congregation reflected the diversity of the surrounding culture as Hellenists (Greek-speaking Jews or Jews who lived by Greek
customs) and Hebrews (more conservative Jews) were members of this community of faith. A
concern had arisen because the Hellenist widows were not being treated fairly in the daily dis-

tribution of food. Instead of being defined by the Great Commission or the Great Promise, the language of murmuring defined this congregation. In response, the twelve apostles conducted a mission and ministry assessment that resulted in the congregation is living by the biblical principle of *Beyond and Within*:

> Now during those days, when the disciples were increasing in number, the Hellenists complained against the Hebrews because their widows were being neglected in the daily distribution of food. And the twelve called together the whole community of the disciples and said, "It is not right that we should neglect the word of God in order to wait on tables. Therefore, friends, select from among yourselves seven men of good standing, full of the Spirit and of wisdom, whom we may appoint to this task, while we, for our part, will devote ourselves to prayer and to serving the word." What they said pleased the whole community, and they chose Stephen, a man full of faith and the Holy Spirit, together with Philip, Prochorus, Nicanor, Timon, Parmenas, and Nicolaus, a proselyte of Antioch. They had these men stand before the apostles, who prayed and laid their hands on them. The word of God continued to spread; the number of the disciples increased greatly in Jerusalem, and a great many of the priests became obedient to the faith.

The pressing ministry need of the Jerusalem congregation was equitable care for its members. The pressing mission of the Jerusalem congregation was the fulfillment of the Great Commission and the Great Promise. As the mission and ministry needs of the congregation met, a disagreement arose. Responding to this situation, the apostles modeled a pattern of resolution that still applies to today's congregations:

1) Define the mission of the congregation;

2) Assess current reality through mission values;

3) Organize a response through consultation of leadership;

4) Achieve consensus by the congregation that will lead to the transformation of current reality.

Define the Mission of the Congregation

The apostles clearly defined the mission of the Jerusalem congregation as they summoned the body of disciples and said, "It is not right that we should neglect the word of God in order to wait on tables." Clearly stating that the mission of the congregation was a call beyond internal needs, they created the context in which the dispute within the Jerusalem congregation would be addressed.

Assess Current Reality through Mission Values

Assessing the current reality of the congregation through the mission value of preaching the word of God, the apostles determined that they could not ignore the congregation's internal needs while also fulfilling the mission of the congregation. They also determined that the internal needs of the congregation could not become the focus of the congregation's existence, nor could they become the focus of their ministry.

Organize a Response through Consultation of Leadership

Responding to the reality of the situation, the apostles organized a response. Consulting with the leadership of the congregation, seven deacons were chosen who would oversee the internal needs that had become such a pressing issue. Following this time of mission definition, reality assessment, consultation, and organizing of a response, they reported their response to a congregation that was pleased with what they said.

Achieve Consensus That Will Lead to the Transformation of Current Reality

The result of this pattern of resolution was that the congregation maintained its focus on its reason for existence, resolved its internal ministry needs, and greatly multiplied the number of its disciples. In other words, the current reality within the congregation was transformed as the identity of the congregation was defined through its mission. Unity of vision and consensus of mission replaced the murmuring that could have led this congregation into the wilderness.

Too many congregations face an identity crisis as they struggle with ministry needs that cause them to focus within rather than beyond. Murmuring is the language of these communities of faith as they wander in their search for God's Promised Land for Jesus' disciples. Lacking a unity of vision, their members seek to protect their own turf rather than to live sacrificially for God's kingdom. Cherished memories of the past and cherished ministries of the present occupy the vision of these congregations.

Jesus' second invitation to discipleship can help congregations to live beyond an identity crisis. Accepting the path of discipleship that leads to Calvary and the empty tomb, the identity of congregations can be transformed. Living by the biblical principle of *Beyond and Within*, congregations can live into a new reality as they seek to fulfill the Great Commission and the Great Promise. Reflecting and assessing, organizing, and achieving congregational consensus, they can live into a new identity by glorifying God as Jesus' sent people into the world.

God's Promised Land for a local church is realized in the unity of vision for ministry that empowers that congregation to live as faithful disciples of Jesus Christ. There is no possibility for a local church to unite in ministry until a congregation of Jesus' disciples discerns and lives a ministry that reflects God's mission. In order to discern God's vision for ministry in the life of a congregation, that community of Christian disciples must be willing to reflect upon the message of Jesus that guides it to a calling beyond itself.

A vision that nurtures and equips people to look beyond their self-focused concerns defines effective ministry in churches that are bound for the Promised Land of discipleship. Remembering Jesus' admonition to take up their cross, they share the love of God by focusing on the sending love of God that led Jesus to the cross. Understanding that the cross of Jesus

Christ transforms their vision of ministry, they look within their community of faith at those things that are hindering them from living as God's called people. Guided by the biblical principle of *Beyond and Within,* they model the envisioned reality of God's Promised Land of discipleship as the focus of their congregation shifts from the past to the future. Understanding that the context of following Jesus to Calvary and to the empty tomb frames Jesus' invitation of the cross, they know that the journey of discipleship is always a journey beyond the present context of their church's life. Realizing that Jesus' crucifixion and resurrection fully reveal the truth of God's kingdom, they have accepted Jesus' second invitation to discipleship.

This is God's Promised Land for Jesus' disciples. This is God's Promised Land for your church. Are you ready to enter this Promised Land?

Praying Together

> Lord of new life, through your crucifixion and resurrection you define our lives as disciples. It is only in you that we find our meaning and can be transformed into your likeness. As we continue our journey to your Promised Land, awaken us to the promise of your Holy Spirit that we may be witnesses to the world of your transforming love and seek to be of service to others more than to ourselves. Amen.

Seeking God's Vision Together

The following questions provide an opportunity for personal and group reflection as your church seeks God's vision. The three types of questions will lead you to:

- *Reflect on the scripture passages of the study (Questions for Scriptural Reflection);*
- *Express your opinions regarding the current reality of your church (Helping Your Voice To Be Heard);*
- *Participate thought and conversation (Questions for Reflection and Discussion).*

Questions for Scriptural Reflection

From the scriptural text in this chapter, reflect on the following questions and answers

1. What was the same in Jesus' two invitations to discipleship?

   Mark 1:17, Mark 8:34: Both invitations included a call to follow.

2. What was the difference in Jesus' two invitations to discipleship?

   The reality of discipleship had changed. Jesus' first invitation in Mark 1:17 was for the disciples to be fishers of people. Jesus' second invitation in Mark 8:34 was for the disciples to take up their cross.

3. How do the Great Commission of Matthew 28:16-20 and the Great Promise of Acts 1:8 define the existence of the church?

   Both the Great Commission and the Great Promise define the existence of the church by Jesus' as they call disciples to a life of faith in a crucified and risen Lord.

4. How did the apostles assess the current reality of the Jerusalem church?

   Acts 6:2: They assessed the internal need of the congregation through the mission of the congregation.

5. What is the pattern of conflict resolution that the Jerusalem church practiced?
   a. *Acts 6:2: Define the mission of the congregation.*
   b. *Acts 6:1-2: Assess current reality through mission values.*
   c. *Acts 6:3-4: Organize a response through consultation with leadership.*
   d. *Acts 6:5-7: Achieve consensus by the congregation that will enable current reality to be transformed.*

Helping Your Voice To Be Heard

Responses to these questions will formulate information that will allow your church to make intentional decisions about the mission and ministry of your life together. Please enter your responses in the corresponding section of the response sheet provided with this study book. Each answer should be your initial response.

1. Your church's approach to ministry and mission is focused on:
   a. Beyond;
   b. Within.

2. Do disagreements within your congregation tend to:
   a. Be resolved in ways that are effective?
   b. Be resolved in ways that cause discord?

3. Disagreements at our church are usually:
   a. Resolved quickly by consensus;
   b. Resolved quickly by one or two key leaders;
   c. Resolved quickly by the pastor or church staff;
   d. Avoided and unresolved.

4. Do you believe your church practices the pattern of conflict resolution that was practiced by the Jerusalem church?
   a. Yes;
   b. No.

5. Is your church united in its vision?
   a. Yes;
   b. No.

6. Does your congregation clearly understand its mission?
   a. Yes;
   b. No.

7. Disagreements in your church tend to:
   a. Linger;
   b. Be discussed openly;
   c. Cause hard feelings;
   d. Help your congregation to understand more clearly its mission;
   e. Polarize your congregation;
   f. Lead to new ways of thinking;
   g. Lead to new ministries;
   h. Result in blaming and frustration;
   i. Result in God's love being seen.

8. Do current ministries in your church invite people to see beyond self-focused concerns?
   a. Yes;
   b. No;
   c. Don't know.

Questions for Reflection and Discussion

The answers to the following questions provide an opportunity for personal and group reflection as your church seeks God's vision. These questions will help you know more about your church and each other.

1. What programs/ministries take precedence at your church? Discuss whether they focus *beyond* your church or focus *within* your church.

2. Discuss the difference between Jesus' initial invitation for his disciples to follow him and his second invitation for his disciples to follow him.

3. What does Jesus mean when he says, "If any want to become my followers, let them deny themselves and take up their cross and follow me"?

4. Why does your church exist?

5. What would a vision based on the concept of *Beyond and Within* look like for your church?

Entering God's Promised Land

Jesus has prayed for your church. Your community of faith can enter God's Promised Land for Jesus' disciples. Joy and unity can be the songs of faith sung in your congregation. God can be glorified through your church's ministry and mission. Your church has a prayer for living in the envisioned reality that Paul described for the church in Philippians 2:1-4:

> If then there is any encouragement in Christ, any consolation from love, any sharing in the Spirit, any compassion and sympathy, make my joy complete: be of the same mind, having the same love, being in full accord and of one mind. Do nothing from selfish ambition or conceit, but in humility regard others as better than yourselves. Let each of you look not to your own interests, but to the interests of others.

The community of Jesus' disciples at Philippi formed the first church that Paul had planted on European soil. They held a special place of joy in Paul's heart as witnessed by Paul's words of greeting to them in the beginning of this letter in Philippians 1:3-5:

> I thank my God every time I remember you, constantly praying with joy in every one of my prayers for all of you, because of your sharing in the gospel from the first day until now.

To understand the impact of Paul's thankful prayer, we need to understand the reality in which he wrote his letter. Paul is in prison awaiting trial for preaching the gospel of Christ. Some people in the Church at Philippi have used Paul's imprisonment to advance their own concerns. Affection for what Paul had made possible in the formation of their community of faith has guided other people in the church. In the midst of these two realities, Philippians 1:15-18 records Paul's expression of gratitude that the church continues to proclaim Christ:

> Some proclaim Christ from envy and rivalry, but others from goodwill. These pro-claim Christ out of love, knowing that I have been put here for the defense of the gospel; the others proclaim Christ out of selfish ambition, not sincerely but intend-ing to increase my suffering in my imprisonment. What does it matter? Just this, that Christ is proclaimed in every way, whether out of false motives or true; and in that I rejoice.

What allowed Paul to rejoice, even though he knew some people were using his imprison-ment to advance their own agendas? Why was Paul thankful as he wrote from a prison cell? Paul was able to rejoice and be thankful because he had entered God's Promised Land for Jesus' dis-ciples. Paul glorified God because his life had become a song of faith to Jesus. He was living in an envisioned reality formed by the truth of a Savior who can redeem a prison cell and per-sonal agendas. Paul rejoiced and was thankful because he had become the servant of all as he followed Jesus in the call of discipleship that leads to the cross of Calvary and the reality of the empty tomb. It was the reality of the servant ministry of Christ that Paul envisioned as he encouraged the Philippians to nurture each other in faith by doing nothing from selfishness or conceit, in humility counting others better than themselves, looking not only to their own interests, but also to the interests of others. To help the members of the Church at Philippi understand how they could live in the reality of this Promised Land of discipleship, Paul fol-lowed his words about the envisioned reality of Philippians 2:1-4 with the words of one of the ancient songs of Christianity in Philippians 2:5-11:

> Let the same mind be in you that was in Christ Jesus, who, though he was in the form of God, did not regard equality with God as something to be exploited, but emptied himself, taking the form of a slave, being born in human likeness. And being found in human form, he humbled himself and became obedient to the point of death—even death on a cross. Therefore God also highly exalted him and gave him the name that is above every name, so that at the name of Jesus every knee should bend, in heaven and on earth and under the earth, and every tongue should confess that Jesus Christ is Lord, to the glory of God the Father.

This ancient praise of God affirms the self-emptying love that empowered Jesus to become the least of all and the servant of all through the cross. Known as the "kenosis hymn" (a Greek word that means self-emptying), the words of this song of praise witness to the deliberate choices of self-emptying love that defined the nature of Jesus as he walked the path of the cross. As important as the words of the "kenosis hymn" are in understanding the nature of Jesus, they are equally important in understanding the nature of Christ's body.

If a congregation is going to enter God's Promised Land of discipleship, its members must intentionally choose to empty themselves of their own agendas as they take on the nature and mission of Jesus Christ. Rather than being driven by the human need to win, the redeemed need to serve leads them. Singing the redeeming song of God's faithfulness, congregations are transformed occurs through the power of Christ's servant nature. This unified song of redemption is not easy to learn or sing. It requires members of a congregation to define their lives by humility as they look out for the interests of others. Rather than seeking the self-preservation of personal interests, members of a transformed congregation understand that self-emptying love defines their response to Christian discipleship. Instead of being a collection of dissonant voices that seek to preserve cherished memories of the past or cherished ministries of the present, a transformed congregation looks beyond itself to the power of the cross of Jesus Christ. Singing in the harmony of servant faith, a congregation is transformed when its members have the mind of Christ among them.

In learning to sing this song of faithfulness, a congregation must trust in the wisdom of God that shapes its identity as it looks beyond the past and the present and into the future God has promised. When the mission of Jesus' prayer for his disciples defines a congregation, its ministries equip people to become followers of Jesus sent into the world. Just as Jesus was identified by the deliberate choices that empowered him to take the form of a servant, congregations bound for God's Promised Land are identified by the deliberate choices that empower servant ministry. They make intentional decisions about their nature and mission. Ministry decisions are not top-down mandates from congregational leadership, nor are they momentary responses of emotions that are not connected to the overall vision of the congregation. Instead, decisions are made as right questions are asked: questions about Christian discipleship, questions about the nature and mission of a local congregation, questions about giants that are facing a congregation, questions about servant ministry as a congregation focuses beyond itself, and questions about the power of the cross of Jesus. As members of a congregation hear the right questions, they are able to discern and move toward the same vision of discipleship. They accomplish this as they encourage one another and participate as a community of faith united by God's Holy Spirit. In turn, as the mind of Christ defines the nature and mission of a congregation, people beyond the congregation will begin asking questions about the transformation that is occurring. Through these questions, they will be drawn to the power of God they are witnessing through the ministry of that congregation.

The story of Pentecost is an example of what happens when people sing the song of God's faithfulness through Jesus. This story of the beginning of the church is told in the second chapter of Acts as the disciples, empowered by the Holy Spirit, become apostles (those sent out) by proclaiming the message of God's grace they had witnessed in the life, death, and resurrection of Jesus.

> When the day of Pentecost had come, they were all together in one place. And suddenly from heaven there came a sound like the rush of a violent wind, and it filled the entire house where they were sitting. Divided tongues, as of fire, appeared among them, and a tongue rested on each of them. All of them were filled with the Holy

Spirit and began to speak in other languages, as the Spirit gave them ability. Now there were devout Jews from every nation under heaven living in Jerusalem. And at this sound the crowd gathered and was bewildered, because each one heard them speaking in the native language of each. Amazed and astonished, they asked, "Are not all these who are speaking Galileans? And how is it that we hear, each of us, in our own native language? Parthians, Medes, Elamites, and residents of Mesopotamia, Judea and Cappadocia, Pontus and Asia, Phrygia and Pamphylia, Egypt and the parts of Libya belonging to Cyrene, and visitors from Rome, both Jews and proselytes, Cretans and Arabs—in our own languages we hear them speaking about God's deeds of power." All were amazed and perplexed, saying to one another, "What does this mean?"

As the Holy Spirit danced like wildfire upon the apostles, they began to speak in the languages of people from around the world. This miraculous event signaled the birth of the church. The defining miracle of the church's birth, however, was not that the apostles were able to speak in languages they did not know. The defining miracle of the Church's birth was that people from every nation around the world heard the *same message* of God's grace through Jesus being proclaimed. Upon hearing this message, they, in turn, asked the same question, "what does this mean," as they were drawn to the story of God's love through Jesus. As a result of the same message of God's grace being heard and trusted, the closing verse of the second chapter of Acts records the following: "And day by day the Lord added to their number those who were being saved" (Acts 2:47).

While the story of Pentecost is a miraculous account of the church's birth, it is imperative to remember that the story of Pentecost in Acts 2 is not a solitary event. The story of Jesus' disciples gathering with one accord and devoting themselves in prayer in Acts 1:12-14 precedes Pentecost. The story of how the congregation in Jerusalem defined its nature and mission follows Pentecost.

One story of how the congregation in Jerusalem defined its nature and mission is found in Acts 15 when the apostles made intentional choices about how Gentiles should be recognized as disciples of Jesus. This choice was necessary because some of the members of the Jerusalem church were teaching Gentile Christians in Antioch that they needed to be circumcised according to the custom of Moses in order to be saved. Paul and Barnabas, who were on their first missionary journey, directly confronted and disputed the teachers over this requirement. Unable to settle their differences, Paul, Barnabas, and some other members of their missionary team were appointed to go to Jerusalem to consult with the apostles and elders regarding this dispute. This meeting became known as the Jerusalem Council. At this council, some Pharisee believers said that, in addition to being circumcised, Gentile believers were also required to live by all the customs and requirements of Judaism. This teaching caused much debate, and as a result the church decided that God's grace made no distinction between Gentiles and Jews. With this understanding, Gentile Christians would not have to observe the customs and requirements of Judaism. The church also decided that Gentile Christians, out of respect for Jewish Christians, should live into their new nature as disciples of Jesus by abstaining "only from things polluted by idols and from fornication and from whatever has been strangled and from blood" (Acts 15:20). Both the Jerusalem and the Antioch congregations were in consensus with the decisions of the Jerusalem Council as each congregation redefined its nature in responding to the mission of the church.

In transforming the nature of their congregations, the Jerusalem church and the Antioch church were required to have the mind of Christ among them as they lived by Paul's advice to the Philippians: "Do nothing from selfishness or conceit, but in humility count others better than yourselves. Let each of you look not only to his own interests, but also to the interests of others." Living by this advice, both the Jewish and Gentile Christians lived in the self-emptying love of Jesus as they looked beyond their own interests to the mission of the gospel of Jesus Christ. Entering God's Promised Land for disciples of Jesus, they:

1) Stopped doing what hindered them from looking to the interests of others;

2) Kept doing what gave foundation to their faith;

3) Started new expressions of mission and ministry that defined the mind of Christ that was among them.

Through intentional choices, the Pharisee Christians crucified their requirement for Gentiles to be circumcised and to obey the law of Moses before they could be saved. Through intentional choice, the Gentile Christians crucified their former lifestyles that would keep them from living lives that glorified God. Taking up their crosses, both Jewish and Gentile disciples looked beyond their own concerns as their corporate mission was defined by the cross of Jesus Christ. Understanding their mission was to proclaim the grace of God, the leaders of the Jerusalem and Antioch congregations agreed to let go of what was keeping them from looking to the interest of others.

Their transforming response, however, did not end with this sacrificial step. The redefinition of their nature also required them to determine what they should continue and how they should respond to the dispute that had arisen. The Jewish Christians continued to hold fast to circumcision and the requirements of Judaism while living into a new understanding of God's grace as they accepted Gentile Christians as fellow disciples. The Gentile Christians continued to maintain their identity outside of the requirements of Judaism while living into a new understanding of God's grace as they respected the law and customs of Judaism. Together, they achieved a response that transformed their mission as they witnessed to the grace of God by having the mind of Christ among them. Their faithfulness to this mission allowed them to move beyond conflict resolution to transformation. Looking beyond their human need to win, they looked to the interests of others, continued what gave foundation to their faith, and created new expressions of mission.

To enter God's Promised Land of discipleship, conflict resolution must lead a congregation to an envisioned reality of calling and mission. The transforming traits of Paul's letter to the Philippians define the nature of these congregations: encouragement in Christ, love, participation in the Spirit, affection, sympathy, of the same mind, having the same love, being in full accord. The transforming mind of Christ defines the mission of these congregations as they allow the self-emptying love of Jesus to guide the focus of their life together. They do not wait for crises to occur before change happens. Instead, they live out their calling through an ongoing process of reflection and assessment.

Proactive in achieving congregational consensus, their congregational leaders understand that all organizations go through life cycles. Acknowledging cherished memories of the past and cherished ministries of the present, these congregations are able to respect what gives foundation to the present reality of their faith while focusing beyond the present into God's envisioned reality. Recognizing that ministry choices which led to their present maturity will likely cause them to plateau and begin a stage of decline in their life cycle, their leaders and members consult and create new expressions of ministry that define the mind of Christ among them. Focusing on the interests of others, they look beyond their own interests as they intentionally crucify those things that keep them from growing in their mission of witnessing to the grace of God in Jesus Christ. Persons within these congregations realize that the mind of Christ calls them to transformation.

Congregations that are wandering in their search for God's Promised Land have a different agenda. Their primary mission is to maintain the cherished memories of the past and cherished ministries of the present. Survival, rather than mission, is their focus as they seek to preserve their lives by disconnecting and distancing themselves from the reality of their present possibilities and challenges. Wandering in their search for God's Promised Land, they give witness to their nature in other ways: discouragement, members looking to protect their own interests rather than looking to the interests of others, discord, suspicion of the motives of others, and lack of unity. This wandering search will result in a congregation defined by self-interest, self-focus, and self-concern.

All congregations must make intentional decisions about their nature and mission. Either the envisioned reality of Jesus' prayer for his disciples will define their nature and mission, or a perceived reality that wanders in search of a reason for existence will define them.

For many congregations, entry into the Promised Land for which Jesus prayed will require difficult choices. It will require an honest assessment of the current reality of their church. Faithful reports will be essential from leaders who will survey the reality to which God is calling them. They will need to ask right questions as they organize a response to the giants that they face. Consensus will be required as people in their congregation spiritually engage in the discipline of hearing the same message and asking the same questions. Faithful conversations will be needed as the primary mission of the congregation is determined. Following the model of the Jerusalem Council, these congregations will crucify concerns that hinder them from looking to the interests of others, continue what gives foundation to their faith, and create new expressions of mission and ministry that define the mind of Christ that is among them. They realize that if they are to see with the vision of the risen Christ, they must first look to the cross of the crucified Christ. In doing this, they will live and relate with each other and their surrounding communities in an envisioned reality that glorifies God. They will enter God's Promised Land for Jesus' disciples.

May God bless your church on your journey to this Promised Land.

Praying Together

Christ of every age, your prayers go before us. As we hear and respond to the message of your grace, your power enables us to overcome the challenges of this world. As we follow your example, we become unified in our witness. As we continue our journey to your Promised Land, grant us humble hearts so that we might make right decisions that lead us there. We pray that all we do will glorify your name in all the earth. Amen.

Seeking God's Vision Together

The following questions provide an opportunity for personal and group reflection as your church seeks God's vision. The three types of questions will lead you to:

- *Reflect on the scripture passages of the study (Questions for Scriptural Reflection);*
- *Express your opinions regarding the current reality of your church (Helping Your Voice To Be Heard);*
- *Participate in thought and conversation (Questions for Reflection and Discussion).*

Questions for Scriptural Reflection

From the scriptural texts in this chapter, reflect on the following questions and answers:

1. What are the characteristics of a church that is living in the envisioned reality for which Jesus prayed?

   Philippians 2:1-4: Encouragement in Christ, being of the same mind, having the same love, being in full accord and of one mind, doing nothing from selfishness or conceit, humility, looking not only to own interests but also to the interests of others.

2. Why did God exalt Jesus?

   Philippians 2:5-11: Jesus did not count equality with God as the goal of his life. Jesus became a servant, humbling himself, as he obediently shared the message of God's love even when his obedience led to the cross.

3. What is the significance of Pentecost in the history of the church?

Acts 2:1-11: Pentecost is the story of the church's birth. It is the story of how the Holy Spirit empowered the disciples to become apostles as they told about the grace of God they had witnessed in the life, death, and resurrection of Jesus. Pentecost is the day that people from around the world heard the same message about Jesus and asked the same question about Jesus.

4. How did the Jerusalem Council model conflict resolution that was transformational?

Acts 15: People were willing to look to the interests of others, continue what gave foundation to their faith, and create new expressions of mission and ministry that defined the mind of Christ that was among them.

Helping Your Voice To Be Heard

Responses to these questions will formulate information that will allow your church to make intentional decisions about the mission and ministry of your life together. Please enter your responses in the corresponding section of the response sheet provided with this study book. Each answer should be your initial response.

1. When our church has to make a choice, we:
   a. Are guided by a unified vision;
   b. Get bogged down in details.

2. Our church makes intentional decisions about its ministries and mission:
   a.   Yes;
   b.   No;
   c.   Don't know.

3. Once the church makes a decision, the tendency in our church is for people to:
   a.   Harbor hard feelings;
   b.   Work behind the scenes creating discord;
   c.   Support church decisions they may not personally agree with;
   d.   Create factions of self-interest;
   e.   Define decisions as winning or losing.

4. Are there new expressions of ministry in your church?
   a.   Yes;
   b.   No;
   c.   Don't know.

5. Most of our church programs focus on:
   a.   The needs of our members;
   b.   The needs of our surrounding community.

6. Our church is mainly concerned with:

a.   Mission;

b.   Survival.

7. I believe that because Jesus has prayed for our church, our church has a prayer and can enter God's Promised Land for Jesus' disciples:

a.   Yes;

b.   No.

Questions for Reflection and Discussion

The answers to the following questions provide an opportunity for personal and group reflection as your church seeks God's vision. These will help you know more about your church and each other.

1. How can a church glorify God?

2. How can your life glorify God?

3. Why was Paul thankful as he wrote from a prison cell?

4. How have you seen the "kenosis" (self-emptying) love of Jesus in your church?

5. Can you think of a time in your life or in your church when conflict resolution led to transformation?

Bible Study Response Sheets

Bible Study One: Does Your Church Have a Prayer?

1. Would you consider your church to be a praying church?
   a. _____ Yes;
   b. _____ No.

2. Is your church a joyful place?
   a. _____ Yes;
   b. _____ No.

3. Does a common vision that glories God unite your church?
   a. _____ Yes;
   b. _____ No.

4. Do people believe in Jesus because of your church?
   a. _____ Yes;
   b. _____ No.

5. Does your church make God's love known?
   a. _____ Yes;
   b. _____ No.

6. Does your church have a vision/mission statement?
   a. _____ Yes;
   b. _____ No;
   c. _____ Don't know.

7. If your church has a mission statement, do you think it reflects the mission of Jesus' prayer for his disciples as noted in question three of "Questions for Scriptural Reflection"?
   a. _____ Yes;
   b. _____ No.

8. Which question would generate the most discussion at your church?
   a. _____ Who has the keys to which doors at your church?
   b. _____ How can we open the doors of our church to our community?

Bible Study Two: What Reality Do You Choose?

1. I have observed murmuring in our church and have found it to be:
   a. _____ Significantly detrimental;
   b. _____ Somewhat detrimental;
   c. _____ Minimally detrimental;
   d. _____ Not at all detrimental.

2. Does your church have a history of honestly assessing its current reality?
   a. _____ Yes;
   b. _____ No;
   c. _____ Don't know.

3. Issues at your church are decided through:
   a. _____ Envisioned reality;
   b. _____ Perceived reality.

4. Your church's past experience and history:
   a. _____ Hold you back;
   b. _____ Move you forward.

5. Today in our church:
   a. _____ Most people choose to focus on the challenges that are facing our church as the ten spies did;
   b. _____ Most people choose to focus on the promise of God's presence for our church like Joshua and Caleb.

6. Does your church understand that it stands on the edge of God's Promised Land for Jesus' disciples?
   a. _____ Yes;
   b. _____ No;
   c. _____ Don't know.

Bible Study Three: Overcoming Giants

1. Can your church name the giants that are preventing you from entering God's Promised Land of joy and unity?
   a. _____ Yes;
   b. _____ No.

2. Does your church focus more on the giants that are facing it than on God's vision for the future?
   a. _____ Focus more on the giants;
   b. _____ Focus more on God's vision for the future.

3. Has your church demonstrated the courage to make intentional choices that will empower it to overcome the giants that are facing it?
   a. _____ Yes;
   b. _____ No.

4. Would your community consider your church to be relevant to the present challenges of life?
   a. _____ Yes;
   b. _____ No;
   c. _____ Don't know.

5. What are the current giants that are facing your church?
   a. _____ Lack of age diversity in the congregation;
   b. _____ A changing neighborhood;
   c. _____ Financial challenges;
   d. _____ Aging facility;
   e. _____ Changes in the number of church members;
   f. _____ Worship attendance;
   g. _____ History of conflict;
   h. _____ Other (List responses below).

   _____

   _____

6. What are strengths within your congregation that can help your church to overcome the giants it faces?
   a. _____ Worship;
   b. _____ Location;
   c. _____ Spiritual formation opportunities;
   d. _____ Mission;
   e. _____ Church facility;
   f. _____ Financial strength;
   g. _____ Communication.

Bible Study Four: Asking the Right Questions

1. Would you say that "hallway conversations" at your church are usually meant to:
   a. _____ Gain understanding;
   b. _____ Complain;
   c. _____ Resolve conflict;
   d. _____ Accuse and blame.

2. Do questions in your church tend to:
   _____ Build community;
   _____ Destroy relationships.

3. Jesus asked his disciples, "What were you discussing on the way?" What does your church spend time discussing? (Pick four.)
   a. _____ Present ministries;
   b. _____ The past;
   c. _____ Future ministries;
   d. _____ Who Jesus is;
   e. _____ Who's right or who's wrong;
   f. _____ Spreading the Good News;
   g. _____ What happened on Sunday;
   h. _____ Finances;
   i. _____ Lay leadership;
   j. _____ Staff leadership;
   k. _____ Concerns of your church;
   l. _____ Concerns of your community;
   m. _____ Defining your church's ministry;
   n. _____ Long-term survival;

    o.   _____ Disappointing ministries;

    p.   _____ Successful ministries;

    q.   _____ How to get more people involved;

    r.   _____ Worship attendance;

4. What labels have you heard in your church? (Pick three.)

    a.   _____ Those new members;

    b.   _____ Those old timers;

    c.   _____ Us;

    d.   _____ Them;

    e.   _____ Involved;

    f.   _____ Uninvolved;

    g.   _____ Committed;

    h.   _____ Non committed.

5. Does your congregation focus on:

    a.   _____ Power struggles;

    b.   _____ Ministry.

6. Does your church have questions about its future?

    a.   _____ Yes;

    b.   _____ No;

    c.   _____ Don't know.

7. Do questions in your church invite dialogue from diverse opinions?

    a.   _____ Yes;

    b.   _____ No;

    c.   _____ Don't know.

8. Does the history of your church reflect power struggles that it continues to repeat?

    a.   _____ Yes;

    b.   _____ No;

    c.   _____ Don't know.

9. Is there agreement or disagreement about what your congregation values most?

    a.   _____ Agreement;

    b.   _____ Disagreement;

    c.   _____ Don't know.

Bible Study Five: Beyond and Within

1. Your church's approach to ministry is focused on:
   a. _____ Beyond;
   b. _____ Within.

2. Do disagreements within your congregation tend to:
   a. _____ Be resolved in ways that are effective?
   b. _____ Be resolved in ways that cause discord?

3. Disagreements at our church are usually:
   a. _____ Resolved quickly by consensus;
   b. _____ Resolved quickly by one or two key leaders;
   c. _____ Resolved quickly by the pastor or church staff;
   d. _____ Avoided and unresolved.

4. Do you believe your church practices the pattern of conflict resolution that was practiced by the Jerusalem church?
   a. _____ Yes;
   b. _____ No.

5. Is your church united in its vision?
   a. _____ Yes;
   b. _____ No.

6. Does your congregation clearly understand its mission?
   a. _____ Yes;
   b. _____ No.

7. Disagreements in your church tend to:
   a. _____ Linger;
   b. _____ Be discussed openly;
   c. _____ Cause hard feelings;
   d. _____ Help your congregation to understand more clearly its mission;
   e. _____ Polarize your congregation;
   f. _____ Lead to new ways of thinking;
   g. _____ Lead to new ministries;
   h. _____ Result in blaming and frustration;
   i. _____ Result in God's love being seen.

8. Do current ministries in your church invite people to see beyond self-focused concerns?
   a. _____ Yes;
   b. _____ No;
   c. _____ Don't know.

Bible Study Six: Entering God's Promised Land

1. When our church has to make a choice, we:
   a. _____ Are guided by a unified vision;
   b. _____ Get bogged down in details.

2. Our church makes intentional choices about its ministries and mission:
   a. _____ Yes;
   b. _____ No;
   c. _____ Don't know.

3. Once the church makes a decision, the tendency in our church is for people to:
   a. _____ Harbor hard feelings;
   b. _____ Work behind the scenes creating discord;
   c. _____ Support church decisions they may not personally agree with;
   d. _____ Create factions of self-interest;
   e. _____ Define decisions as winning or losing.

4. Are there new expressions of ministry in your church?
   a. _____ Yes;
   b. _____ No;
   c. _____ Don't know.

5. Most of our church programs focus on:
   a. _____ The needs of our members;
   b. _____ The needs of our surrounding community.

6. I believe that because Jesus prayed for our church, our church has a prayer and can enter God's Promised Land for Jesus' disciples:
   a. _____ Yes;
   b. _____ No.